Walworth Memories

DARREN LOCK & MARK BAXTER

AMBERLEY

Acknowledgements

I dedicate this third book to my goddaughter Bunny and her brother Floyd, to Nelly Lock and to everyone living in Walworth today – hello to the old and new of SE17! Also, a special thank you to all the members of the 'Now And Then Walworth' Facebook page. Thank you for sharing your memories.

Bax

I would like to thank Kevin Mullins, Angelina Long and family, Ernest and Kate and family, Emma Crane and family, Mr George Petts, Maurice Haben and family, Lisa and crew, Mary Millie Rene and Lenny, Pickle and Daisy.
P.S. This one is for you mum x

Darren

First published 2014

Amberley Publishing
The Hill, Stroud
Gloucestershire, GL5 4EP

www.amberley-books.com

British Library Cataloguing in Publication Data.
A catalogue record for this book is available from the British Library.

ISBN 978 1 4456 3449 4 (print)
ISBN 978 1 4456 3457 9 (ebook)

Typesetting and Origination by Amberley Publishing.
Printed in the UK.

Contents

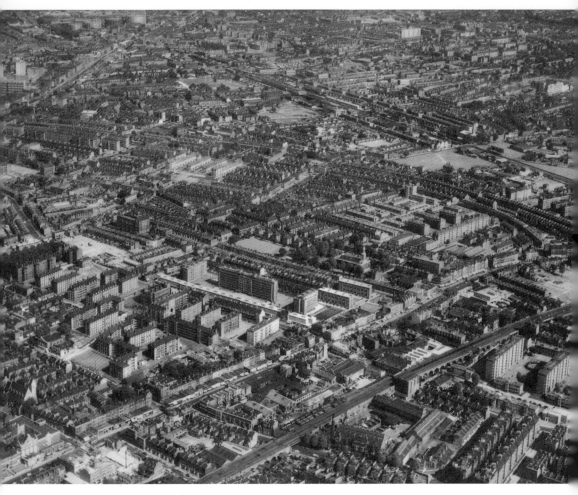

Walworth from the air, *c.* 1960s.

Introduction

When we first mentioned the idea of writing a book on the area of Walworth in 2009, only a few people liked the idea. 'It'll never sell', they said. 'Besides, there isn't a bookshop in the area – no one would buy it.' Well, with the help of local historian Stephen Humphreys, Darren Lock and myself ignored all that, and the good people at Amberley published *Walworth Through Time* in 2010.

As we suspected, the people who once called Walworth their home, together with those who are still very much part of this vibrant neighbourhood, got fully behind the book and it sold in decent numbers. A couple of retailers on the Walworth Road also did their bit and, at one time, the book was available in a bespoke tailors, a newsagent and the pie and mash shop, Arments, where it did a roaring trade. 'I'll have a double, double and a copy of the book please', was a regular food order.

The book was so popular, in fact, that Amberley came back for more and we wrote a second volume – *A Second Selection*. Once again, the support was overwhelming and we had a great community occasion at the launch of the book in the lovely St Peter's church on Liverpool Grove.

Now we have *Walworth Memories*. Using as many unpublished and rarely seen photographs as possible, this time we have let the people of the area – past and present – speak. Some are lifelong residents of SE17 and have never moved. Others have long since left the area, but fondly remember it, and that comes across in their words. We also have more recent arrivals telling us all what they love about this often overlooked part of town. They all have a story to tell.

We dedicate our work on this book to Ellen May Lock, mother of Darren. Nelly, as she was better known, was born in SE17 in 1928. She lived, married, raised a family and died in Walworth. She left us on 4 January 2014, just as we were preparing to put this book together. We hope that with the help of the good people of this manor, we have produced something that is a fitting tribute to a lovely lady.

Viva Walworth. SE17 forever!

Chapter One

The Barrers of the Walworth Road

The Pet Shop – Westmoreland Road
A shop with a stall out front that was in Westmoreland Road for many years. Birds, goldfish, dogs, rabbits, hamsters and much more were for sale.

'Brilliant! I loved that pet shop. I got my cat Bonnie from there. She was a well travelled cat and went from Walworth to Dagenham every weekend in my bag on the tube in the '60s! And she lived 'till she was twenty-three!' (Maggie Webb)

'My Nan and Granddad bought a black and white tabby from there, and called it Nick. The cat lived his later years in Royal Tunbridge Wells and the "posh" life ensured he lived to the ripe old age of twenty-eight.' (Peter Minter)

'I sent my husband out for a pint of milk in Westmoreland Road and he came back with a puppy!' (Rita Beales-Welch)

'It was on the corner of Queens Row and Westmoreland Road. Out the back in the yard, there was a huge tin bath that had goldfish in it. They used to buy the jam jars to use for when someone bought a goldfish. Does anyone remember when all the grass snakes escaped and tried to get out of the shop through the air vents?' (Allen Kilkell)

'I remember this shop. I used to love going inside to have a look. I know it's a pet shop, but it did have a smell about it that was like no other shop I've ever been to. I'll never forget it! Memories eh? The good old days!' (Princess Millies)

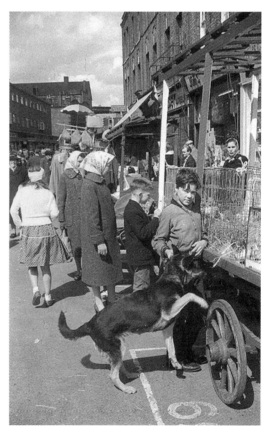

Sarsaparilla – The Drink of the Walworth Road

This 'root' drink is synonymous with SE17. You either bought from Baldwin's the Herbalist on the road itself, or maybe off George Barnes, who had a 'sarse' stall on East Lane for many years and who is fondly remembered.

'I remember this so well, cold in the summer, so hot in the winter. It was lovely. Nice memories.' (Susan Territt)

'The roots of sarsaparilla (locally known as Nannari roots) are also the key ingredient in a popular summer drink in South India. The drink concentrate, commonly referred to as Nannari Sherbet, is made by slightly crushing the roots of sarsaparilla and steeping it in hot water to infuse the flavors. Nannari roots are termed to have medicinal properties and are typically sold in Ayurvedic stores in India.' (Ron Smith)

'George Barnes was a lovely man. He was part of my childhood. His stall epitomised "East Lane" and, for me, was the single point of difference from all the other markets. East Street without sarsaparilla is like the tower without the raven.' (Tina Read Ramus)

'Hot sarsaparilla in the winter and delicious ice-cold pineapple in the summer. Ooh, I wish I could go "down the lane" once again, though back in the '60s and '70s. I did have hot Sarsaparilla from Baldwin's last night. It was delicious!' (Lynn Bull)

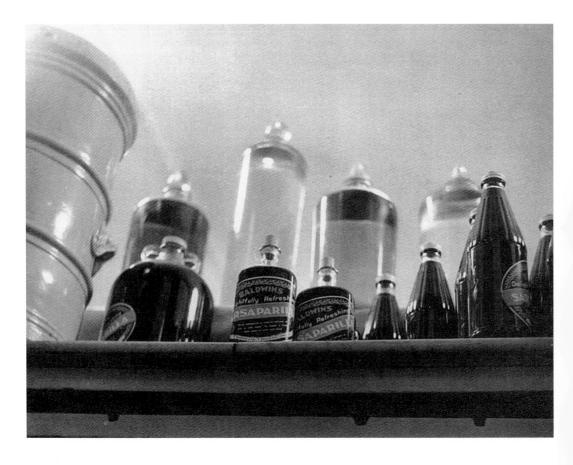

East Street Market – Dawes Street End

East Street Market is one of London's oldest markets. Despite once thriving, in recent years it has seen a sharp decline, a shadow of its former self.

'Brilliant picture! This was when East Lane was a sprawling adventure playground! I once saw John Pertwee in the old indoor antique market. He bought an old church chair. Being an inquisitive boy, I followed him back to his car, which was parked near Rodney Road. He was quite a big TV star at the time.' (Mickey Modern)

'I used to love a rummage on these stalls.' (Margaret Bradford)

'My dad had a stall in there every Sunday with his mate Joe. People also used to sell stuff on the pavement outside; what didn't get sold was left on the floor. Three-card trick merchants were also outside, fascinating to watch.' (Jim Gillingwater)

'Those three-card trick scam men didn't mess about if you started winning. You were told to "wander off" in no uncertain terms.' (Brian Tanner)

'I used to sell stamps with a fella called Frenchy just to the left of them doors there, and a man sold bikes in the kerb across the road on a Sunday morning.' (Mick McConnell)

'My hubby, bless him, didn't have much money, and bought me my first ring here. Really dirty, but his mum gave it a good clean and it turned out to be a gold ruby and diamond Victorian cluster – still wear it today!' (Daryl Chandler)

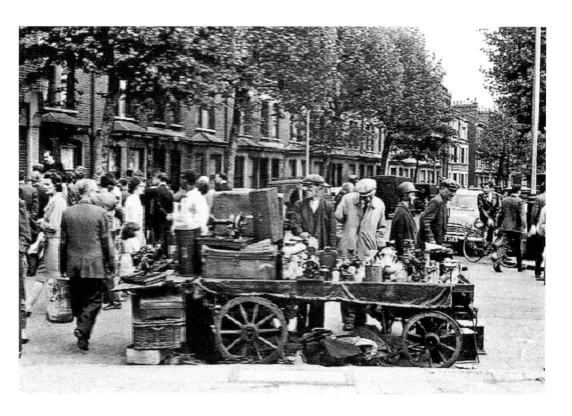

Buskers

The word 'busk' comes from the Spanish *buscar*, which means 'to seek', and street entertainers are always seeking something – be it money or fame. Once a regular sight on many street corners, they are more organised nowadays, often to be found at tube stations or popular tourist destinations.

'A one-man band. Love it!' (Jaime Lynn)

'Who remembers the escapologist who used to do his act on the bombsite at the top of Portland Street and East Street in the early '50s? I used to sit on my dad's shoulders to watch, totally fascinated.' (Margaret Bradford)

'I do! His assistant used to chain him up in a bag and after a struggle, he'd get out. He was always about at Christmas.' (Denis James Kenward)

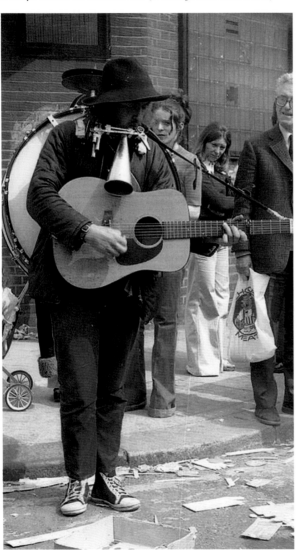

'His name was Alex and he also worked up at Tower Hill. He was a close friend of my dad. Sadly he died in the early '90s.' (Shirley Till)

'I remember the sword he stuck down the middle of the chains!' (Wendy Rodgers Pocknell)

'Anyone remember the chap down the Lane who held a large paving stone on his chest while his chum hit it with a sledgehammer?' (Barbara Brown)

'Remember Earl of Mustard? He was a legendary street dancer of the day. Fascinating to watch and lived to be 97! Can't be bad.' (Maggie Webb)

'All that shuffling must have kept him fit!' (John T. Pettigrew)

'He used to come in the Nelson pub on a Sunday.' (Lee Barber)

Totters

Perhaps better known as rag-and-bone men, they were a very familiar sight only a few years ago, in their horse and carts, ringing their hand bells, looking for anything that was being thrown away. Think Steptoe & Son and you get the picture. The world of recycling, as we know it, really began with these people. The name 'totter' comes from the slang for 'bone', once being 'tot', also the German word for dead.

'I used to help the totters when I was a schoolboy; there were a lot down John Ruskin Street. I used to help the ones down Medlar Street under the arches. I really enjoyed those days.' (William Ogden)

'Remember those yards well. Top of my road was Pelier Street. I remember the lorries parked outside our house with all the rags on.' (Barry Coaker)

'When I was working as a plumber in the Walworth area in the late '70s, I often took lots of scrap metal and copper to Westhall Rag and the metalworks yard in John Ruskin Street.' (John Patrick Fallon)

'Those horses! Poor things stood all day and didn't they stink!' (Jennifer Chesney)

'One of those Totters horses bit me on the arm, right through my new anorak – could have been that one!' (Tim Gillingwater)

'Rag Alley we used to call it down Westmoreland Road on a Sunday morning. And does anyone remember doing the steps with donkey stones? They were first used in textile mills to clean greasy steps, and give them a non-slip finish. Quite often the stones would be given out in exchange for old clothes or scrap metal, by rag totters, or rag-and-bone men as they were sometimes called.' (Valerie Bigsby)

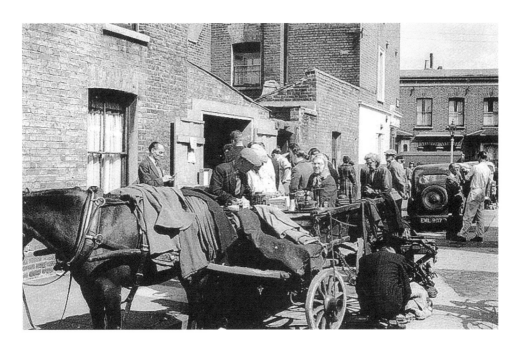

The Good Intent Public House on East Street

Unlike many other well-known pubs in the area, The Good Intent continues to trade in 2014.

'First pub I ever had a beer in was The Good Intent.' (Don Bone)

'You can just see my father-in-law on his flower stall outside The Good Intent. White cap and facing the stall. Bill Tomkins. God rest his soul.' (Karen Tomkins)

'Ah, the Good Intent, where I met my late wife Denise (née Fincken). Thirty-nine years ago this coming New Years Eve.' (Rob Beazley)

'I was treated many a time outside The Good Intent, when the folks went out on coach beanos from there. Picking up the pennies they threw out the coach windows. Oh, they were the days – the early '60s.' (Eddie Moore)

'Lovely picture, brings back a lot of memories. Worked in the shop before you got to Zacks, selling ornaments and bits and pieces. Run by a Jewish family I think. I must have been about twelve or thirteen years old.' (Nicky Edwards)

'My dad had his wake in there in 1969!' (John Cooper)

'The Good Intent! I had my first drink in there with Denise Hall and Antonella Provini – remember Girls? Port and lemon I think!' (Irene Ray)

'This was the '60s. Possibly taken on a weekday market day, as there are no youngsters in this photo. Saturdays and Sundays was packed with girls and boys.' (Joyce Abrahams Rumbol)

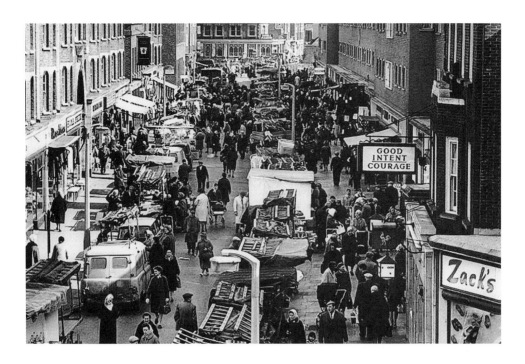

East Street, aka 'The Lane', *c.* 1910

Once the heart and soul of Walworth, it has been struggling over recent years to keep going. It is still fondly thought of and remembered by generations who knew it in its heyday.

'This would have to be a Sunday. All the men and very few women. Sunday was the day men would put on a suit and take a walk down the lane to meet up and catch up. Women were, of course, cooking the dinner...' (Norah Skelton)

'The pubs in East Lane were part of what made it so popular. They all enjoyed good regular customers and plenty of passing trade. Only a couple left now out of five or six.' (Crispin Hudd)

'My great granddad was a "costermonger" and he sold blocks of salt and malt vinegar down the Lane.' (Alexandra Crawley Parker)

'I was the person who convinced Mr Fox to stock Levi's. I sometimes worked there on Sunday mornings. He used to stock copy of Levi's until I told him no self-respecting Mod would wear anything but genuine Levi's! He did good business after that. They were really nice people, and paid me well. He used to stock insipid copies of Fred Perry shirts too. They were a lot cheaper, but my friends and I tried hard to convince him we wouldn't be seen dead in them. One night my mum came rushing into my bedroom saying she heard the smashing of glass, people running and a van pulling away. A bunch of local villains had smashed Fox's window and emptied it. He had to close the side window and put up shutters on the remaining windows. The good old days, ha ha!' (Mickey Modern)

'I can remember those old shops still being there when I went with my Dad on a Sunday morning. He loved going down there. I can remember him and my brother carrying rolls of Lino on their shoulder bought for 2/6*d* per yard and walking from East Lane to the Drovers in the Old Kent Road. Near the gasworks and me walking behind.' (Patricia Lumsden)

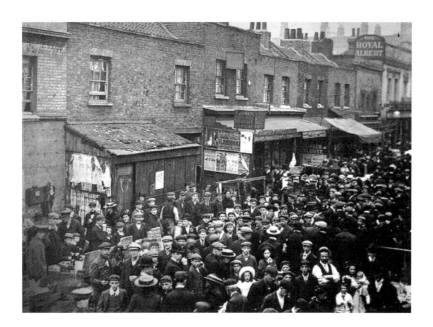

Dawes Street

Overspill from the main street market. Many of the stallholders were 'totters', better known as rag-and-bone men, and would sell directly off the back of their carts, with the horse still attached.

'Looks like an overspill from the flea market. The houses facing were in Dawes Street. Great to see them again. All these buildings look sound. Why oh why did they knock them down? I know cost, but they could have been done up inside and be desirable houses now.' (Maurice Habden)

'Brilliant photo. Agree Maurice, lovely houses, so nice inside they only needed bathrooms and heating. How lovely if they had never been bulldozed our beautiful neighbourly streets. So sad.' (Maggie Webb)

'Oh wow. So nostalgic.' (Betty Lyons)

'Notice all the men in suits.' (Martin Barnett)

'Always very smart then.' (Patricia Gaskin)

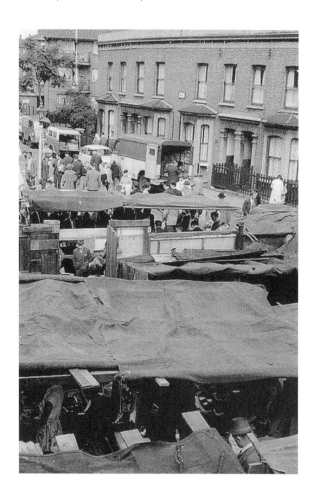

The Tin Huts – East Street Market.
The huts were makeshift shops or stalls where all manner of bric-a-brac could be found and purchased on a Sunday morning.

'Wow! That's an oldie, looks like bike spares. That wasn't about in my day from what I can recall? Most of my trips to the lane would have been during the late '60s to early '80s.' (Karen Richards)

'It was crammed on Sunday mornings, and off into every available side street. You could be lifted, your feet off ground and you'd be carried along.' (Janis McBean)

'Very happy memories. My mum used to be gone for hours down the "lane". She was only going to the corner of King and Queen Street to get some spuds but she'd be chatting for hours. She'd always bump into someone to have a chinwag with, bless her. Then when I was with her she'd always say 'this is my baby' because I was the youngest. Good old days!' (Shirley Till)

'My mum and Nan had a stall there for years, selling second-hand clothes just inside the 1st entrance. I always remember the tea hut and their crusty doorstep bacon sandwiches.' (Tony Williams)

'I used to pull the barrows out before school in the '60s and put away again after school. Happy days.' (Dave Mann)

'What a great picture of East Lane. I grew up in the flats by Pilton Place. I was always awake early from the sounds of the market getting ready.' (Chris Owen)

'Spot the Mosley posters!' (Darren Lock)

'The old bikes were sold in Sandford Row behind the Nelson School and the flea market was next to it on a Sunday. I have a vague recollection of Mosley speaking at the top of Liverpool Grove. Its junction with the Walworth Road there was a regular spot for politicians on their soapboxes.' (Richard Mann)

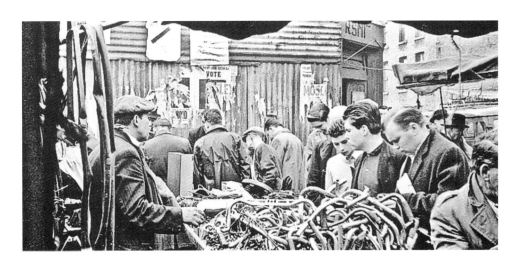

Chapter Two

Hi De Hi

Leysdown-on-Sea, 1964

A popular holiday destination on the East side of the Isle of Sheppey, in Kent, for many from the Walworth area. Whether you were staying in a caravan, a chalet or even camping, the very name brings back many happy memories.

'That's me in the photo, second left. Sadly only three of us left now. We were staying in chalets I believe. They were near Park Avenue or Wing Road, took the grandkids there for a day this year and walked to the site.' (Kevin Mullins)

'We stayed at Warden Bay Holiday Camp.' (Michael McClughen)

'My family had chalets on Warden Bay Holiday Camp.' (Viv Walsh)

'What a place. The whole family went every year they used to hire a coach there was so many of us. Fab holidays at Leysdown. Mums, dads, nans, granddads, cousins everybody. It was a great time in my life. We all stayed on Hearts Camp.' (John Stanley)

'My parents had a caravan there. I spent every six weeks summer holiday there as a kid.' (Maureen Fenlon)

'Remember Stage 3?' (Donald Brady)

'Stage 3 was where most South Londoners went from April 'till the main holiday season. You would walk in and see most of the people from Walworth!' (Tony Thumwood)

'Had some good times there. Who needed Spain? Not me, then…' (Maurice Haben)

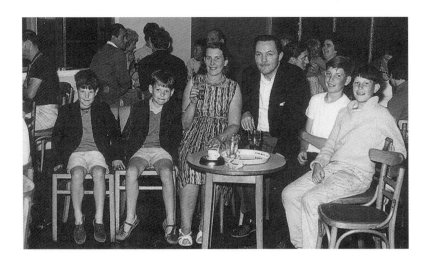

The Isle of Sheppey in the Borough of Swale, Kent
Home to the coastal village of Leysdown, recorded in the Domesday Book as Legesdun – the name derived from the Saxon 'Leswe' meaning pasture and 'Dun' meaning hill. A very popular holiday area for those who lived in Walworth.

'I've had many exotic holidays around the world, but my best memories are when I was a kid down at Sheppey. I was down there when England won the world cup in 1966, what a night in the clubhouse that was.' (Keith Phelby)

'I went to a mate's chalet years ago with a group of friends. One girl called her mum to say she had got there safely and her mum asked her what the time difference was there! We still laugh about that today, twenty-five years later.' (Claire McCabe)

'My grandparents and a few family members had caravans in Eastchurch. I remember there was no indoor loo, and we would either have to make a run for it and leg it to the public brick-built toilets or opt for "nature's toilet"! The van had those dodgy gas lights too.' (Samantha Collins)

'I remember going there in 1967. We had a caravan, and one day there was a terrible storm and we sat and watched the floodwater rushing by! It was frightening. The next day, one field full of caravans looked like a big lake, but we always had a good time.' (Bill Dodd)

'We had a chalet on the Vanity Holiday Camp for over twenty-five years from the '50s. Loved it there, lots of fabulous memories. Like the little dining hall that was next to the Rose and Crown. Delicious homemade food, and I remember the lady who use to sing the bingo numbers out.' (Linda Burgess)

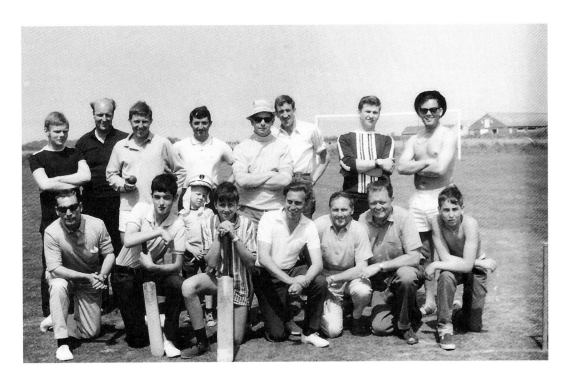

Butlins Holiday Camps

For young families, Butlins offered the perfect two-week escape from the drudgery of the day job. Activities galore, with everything available onsite, you were well and truly catered for.

'Ha ha – that is my dad Stan cheating at the "egg and spoon" race at Butlins. You can take the boy out of South East London, but you can't take South East London out of the boy!' (Jeannie Stanhope)

'Butlins holiday camps used to advertise on telly in the '60s, and their address was in the Walworth Road. I really thought that we could go to this magical place and it was only in the next street, but half knew it wasn't.' (Tim Gillingwater)

'I remember those Butlins adverts; it was the first time I had seen a slide going into the water, I always wanted to go on it! I thought you had to be rich to go on them sort of holidays then ha ha.' (Sharon Roberts)

'I always wanted to go Butlins, but never got there until I was 40! What a let down, Disney it wasn't!' (Rita Beales-Welch)

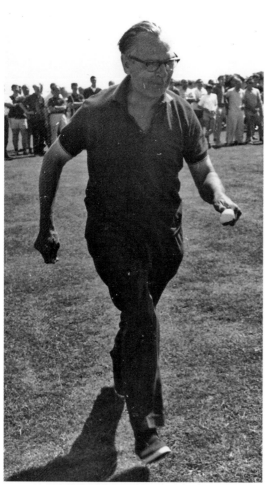

'We went to Butlins at Bognor every year. I thought it was the best place ever!' (Susan Herbert)

'The best bit of the whole day for me was the walk back to the chalet after the evening out in the ball room, bag of chips and a bottle of pop in your hand. Handsome.' (Dave Sainsbury)

'Do you remember the "baby crying in chalet 12" message on the tannoy systems? We used to leave the babies on their own, often with an hankie tied to the door handles, so people knew a kid was inside and to be quiet when passing by! Unbelievable in today's wicked world.' (Bill Bateman)

Banfields Coaches

A very popular choice of vehicle to get you away on your holidays, or that day-trip 'beano' from your pub of choice, or even the away game following Millwall.

'The Banfield flyer!' (Don Bone)

'I think Banfields were in Nunhead Lane? I vaguely remember a booking office in Walworth Road. Even now I remember that smell of warm oil & hot rubber of the tyres. A memory that reminds me of '60/'70s weekends to Leysdown.' (Peter Minter)

'We used to go on days to the seaside with Banfields, picked us by Liverpool Grove.' (Jane Glennie)

'I loved driving the pub beanos to Southend. Plenty of tips from the drunken passengers and, when I cleaned out the coach, plenty of bottles of beer and spirits left behind. Pick up from pub was at 10 a.m., drive straight to Southend, and all coaches had to be out of Southend by 6:00 p.m. We would stop at a pub on the way home 'till closing time. Pubs used to tip us drivers to stop there. Usually got home after midnight, and by the time we got rid of everyone it would be home by 2 a.m.' (Billy Sinclair)

'My family used Charlie Banfields Coaches in the late 1950s for Ramsgate and Margate, wonderful times. We picked up just along from St Peters church, near the wireless rental shop, British Relay.' (Roger Pryor)

'Don't forget away games supporting the mighty Millwall.' (Danny Brown)

'Didn't some of the coaches have small, white, painted numbers on one of the front tyres – roulette style? So when the coach stopped at its destination, the number at the top would win the kitty that the beano mob had put in before leaving?' (Brian Tanner)

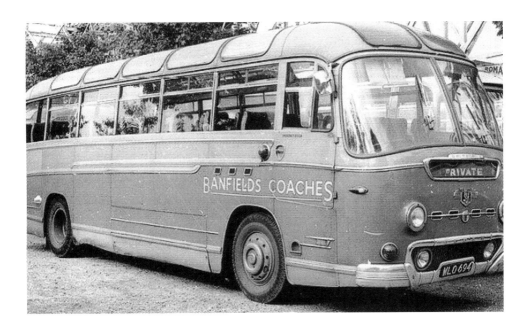

Hop Picking – Various Farms in the Kent Countryside

A working holiday ensured a family got out of their normal surroundings by picking hops for brewing. This was the only trip away most families ever had. Again, they were very fondly remembered.

'I can remember being on the back of a lorry stacked high with boxes, tea chests, ten families going down the Old Kent Road. Out of the smoke and going into the Kent countryside. The air was so clean. My uncle was drunk all the time and he was the driver! The green stain on your hands, the smell of the hops. Close your eyes and go back ... heaven. Loved it!' (Eddie Tume)

'Who had family singing competitions amongst the bins? And who put stones in the bin to make it weigh a bit more?' (Wendy Rodgers Pocknell)

'We went to Goudhurst, loved it. Max Bygraves used to pull down the hops when he was younger and used to pop down there and visit when he became famous. We used to have hot chocolate at night and mum used to make spotted dick in a pot on open fire, it was smashing. The only thing I did not like was the paraffin smell in the huts. But mum used to earn a bit of money that would see us through Xmas.' (Betty Taylor)

'My job was to go to the stand pipes and fill the billy cans up with water so my gran could make the tea.' (Jean Yeo)

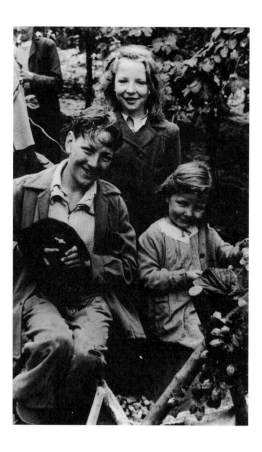

Camping at Hopping

An unknown field in Kent. Many families from SE17 would spend the summer months picking the beer hops as a working holiday. So many stayed in the meagre accommodation offered, mainly sleeping in tents alongside the huts provided.

'Our huts were corrugated iron with wooden doors. Old Mother Butcher used to take her blue kitchen cabinet with her!' (Valerie Bigsby)

'I remember Mum, Dad, aunts, uncles, Nan and Granddad loading up the lorry with furniture from indoors. They made the huts really cosy. My granddad had a piano down there! I can remember all the grown-ups having a good old sing song ... and a crate of light ale.' (Vicky Dennington)

'Too many in our hut most nights, so a couple of us girls kipped in a tent next door!' (Jeannie Stanhope)

'I can remember going with all the family, and we all had hop huts next to each other in Wateringbury, Kent. Straw mattresses and breeze-block walls that didn't go right up to the top, so you could hear everything next door. Always a lovely fire burning outside, which we all used to sit around of a night. Scrumping apples and pears in the day, and washing in cold water. Great fun.' (Susie Wallace)

'I was always falling in the stinging nettles!' (Mary Arnold)

'We went to Horsmonden, on Eastwood's Farm, where my Nan Edie Callaghan had two huts all summer long. Fishing, scrumping, scaring the sheep witless, taking the beer glasses back for the deposit on them whether they were empty or not, the three thimbles trick, the penny up trick, the dug-out khazi. My dad Henry, or his brothers, Mickey, Patsy, Davy Gerry or Bobby singing "In Barefoot Days" and "Abie my Boy". Who doesn't have poignant memoires of hopping, where whole families let their hair down?' (Robert Callaghan)

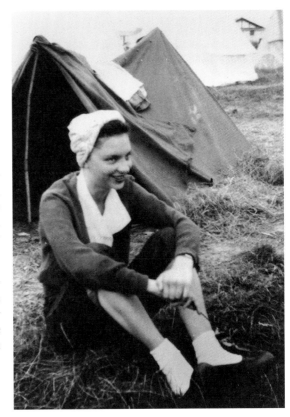

'I remember the long journey southward for our annual holidays to Swanley on the back of a lorry with all the furniture. Now I live there. What a small world.' (Mick and Beryl Collins)

Open-Air Lidos

One of the last remaining outdoor London lidos is at Brockwell Park. Opened in 1937, it is much loved by those who use it, and is often referred to as 'Brixton Beach' due to its close proximity to that area. Hundreds of kids from Walworth would end up here or at Kennington in their summer holidays.

'I remember in the six weeks school holidays. I used to spend nearly every day over there with my mates. Loved it.' (Lesley Tadman)

'Summer Sundays after the pub shut with Mum, Dad, aunts and uncles and all my cousins.' (John Stanley)

'Fffffreeeeeezzzzzing but nonetheless I still learnt to swim there! Happy days.' (Karen Stowell)

'I remember standing on the side and building up my confidence to jump in. And when you did, you came back up very quickly get to the side and get your breath back! Freezing!' (Danny Kaleher)

'They had a little kiosk that sold Bovril even on the hottest day because you still needed that as the water was so cold. I thought the lifeguards had the best job in the world, that's why I became one!' (Sue London)

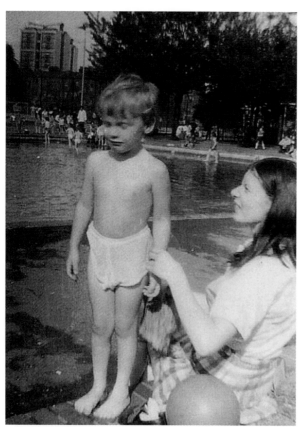

'Anybody remember the push-up lollies from the man with the freezer stand? He had a wonky eye and used to scare me.' (Tony Berkshire)

'I use to love love/hate the Lido, I loved being there with my mates sunning myself in the very warm '70s, but it seemed the hotter the weather the bloody colder the water got. I would dive in and it would take my breath away and I had to get out again.' (Lewis Waite)

'We used to go to The Serpentine during our six weeks holidays. Saw my first Cornetto ice cream there. Very exotic.' (Dave Sainsbury)

Red Bus Rover

A paper 'go anywhere' day bus ticket, in the days of the 'hop on hop off' buses. The ticket was purchased at your local bus garage and you were soon off. For many in Walworth, the West End of London was often the destination of choice, though the more adventurous would venture further afield.

'Remember the red bus rover tickets? You could hop on and off the buses all day long.' (Sammy Legon)

'Been a long time since I've seen one of them.' (Lisa Grace)

'We were always on the red bus rovers as kids, real fun days.' (Vicky Holloway Parsons Rose)

'We always ended up in the West End! Would you let your kids do it now?' (Robert Walters)

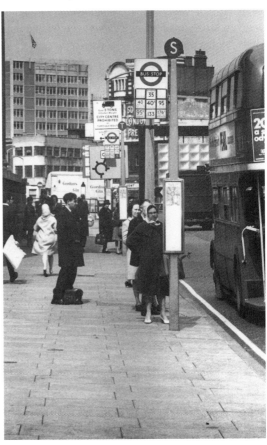

'What a brilliant Saturday game. Sitting there clutching your child red rover. Jump on a bus, sit up front and go all the way to the destination. Then onwards to somewhere "foreign" like Harlesden, Finchley, Clapton Pond. And then it was "how do I get back to Camberwell Green please Mr Conductor, I'm lost!"' (Peter Minter)

'Hamleys, Selfridges, up West. I used to stay on the buses until they went to their destinations, then return back. Talk about mystery tours.' (Danny Walters)

'I was all over London, jumping off one bus and on to another. Sometimes we ended up out in the sticks, not knowing where I was. Usually, it was only Croydon!' (John T. Pettigrew)

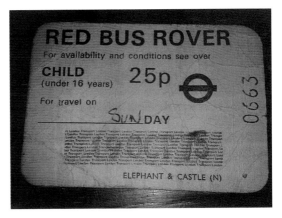

'I loved going right out to the farms and coming home with some veggies for the old mum.' (Alan Murphy)

Chapter Three

Our House

Housekeeping

Once a child was earning wages, it was expected that a portion would be handed over for what was often known as 'board and lodging'. Most people we spoke to think they got a pretty good deal.

'When I first started work in 1955, I gave mum thirty bob – almost half my wages – but she gave me back two shillings a day for my dinner money. Full board with all washing and ironing, plus two bob a day. Pretty good value in my book.' (Alan Barrett)

'Half my wage until I married.' (Linda Wales Callahan)

'I began work on my fifteenth birthday as a trainee secretary. I gave my unopened wage packet of £3.15 to my mum and I was given one pound back. I was in the pub Friday night, had my hair done Saturday at Ambrose at The Elephant, then walked to Eat Lane where I bought black nylons. Then up to Wimbledon Palais on Saturday night and then spent Sunday afternoon at The Lyceum. Got home with not a penny for the week ahead.' (Suzann Waite)

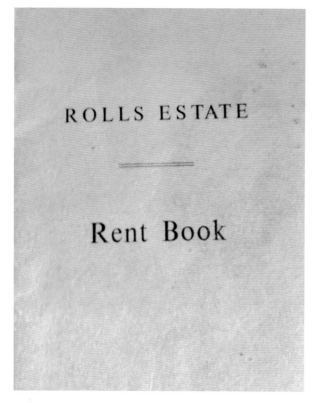

ROLLS ESTATE

Rent Book

'In 1964 I earned £6 1s 5d. I gave my mum £3 10s and she gave me 2s 6d a day back for my lunch and did my washing cooking ironing etc. Bless her.' (Chris Capon)

'I earned four guineas and gave me mum £2 10s of that. I still had enough to go dancing at The Lyceum, The Locarno, and The Royal AND go down the lane for clothes.' (Maggie Webb)

'I got off fairly lightly by the look of it, giving my mum £2 from my £6 wage in 1961. When my eldest girl started work she earned £400 a month and we took one fifth – £80. We put all of it in a building society and it went towards her wedding.' (Richard Mann)

Darwin Buildings

These Victorian tenement type buildings are fondly remembered. The area is now home to Darwin Court, a sheltered housing complex run by Peabody. It offers secure accommodation for those now in their later years of life.

'I was born in flat 156 then we moved to No. 91, next to Mr and Mrs Swain. I was in the shelter when a bomb hit the building near The Victory pub, during the Second World War. It took part the shelter roof off, and Mr Linney, who lived at No. 89, had his legs trapped under a big lump of concrete.' (John Stanley)

'We lived on the first floor, first bay window. When I was just nineteen, my rent was eleven pounds a week. I loved my first little flat.' (Jackie Thomson)

'I went to Veronica's School in Flint Street and used to hang around that area on dinner break with my friends, and we used to see the boys from Paragon School. I remember in 1975/76 they knocked a load of houses down in that area.' (Ann O'Reilly)

'Just as I remember it. I grew up there and lived at 33 Darwin Street. We used to play run outs in Darwin Court.' (Paula Smith)

'I went to Walworth School and my close friend there was Minnie Drury. She lived there with her mum and dad in Darwin Buildings.' (Suzanne Waite)

'Where I grew up. My soul is there more than anywhere else. I still go there in dreams.' (Kay Rogers)

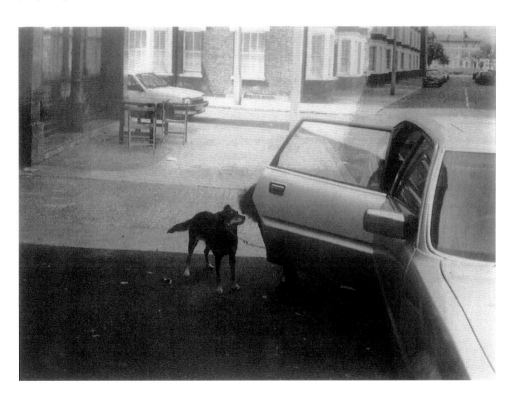

Prefab Housing

Prefabricated houses were built in large numbers as temporary replacement housing stock, due to bomb damage during the Second World War. They were intended for short-term use, but many were still inhabited decades after the end of the war, many in South East London.

'I begged my mum and dad to let us move into one. I think there are still some left in the Catford area. I would love to try and live in one.' (Clare McCabe)

'What is it?' (Lucinda Ball)

'It's prefab housing. Just like a bungalow, all on one level. I lived in one in Wooler Street. It was wonderful; we had garden front and back. My mum was forever telling me to get off the roof! They knocked them down to make way for the building of Aylesbury Estate, great memories.' (Pamela Skipp)

'We lived in one on Morecombe Street, off of the Lane.' (James White)

'Two were built in a space in the middle of a terrace, where I lived in Sedan Street. They took the place of two houses bombed during the war.' (Pauline Ranson Cook)

'My dad's mate lived in one with his missus and daughter and two fully grown Great Danes.' (Yvonne Stevens)

'My friend lived in one just off Secretan Road; apparently they were only built to last ten years. There are still some up forty years later!' (Elaine Wright)

'I lived in one at 98 Wooler Street in the late '50s. I loved it there. I would live in one now.' (Doreen Wickendon)

'Anyone remember when a complete Prefab was nicked from Jardin Street off Neate Street? It was a standing joke at the GLC housing office that it became a holiday home on Sheppey.' (Chas Wood)

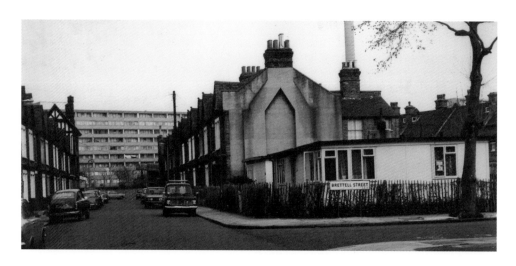

The Aylesbury Estate

A housing estate tarnished with a poor reputation, which hasn't always reflected the good people that live there. It has been in the news recently, when a Channel 4 programme *Ident*, which portrayed the estate as unloved and rubbish strewn, was replaced with one as made by the local Creation Trust led by Charlotte Benstead, which showed a brighter side of life.

'The TV show *The Bill* used to film on the estate and people used to moan about how the place was trashed to make it look more authentic for the stories about prostitutes and drug users. Some locals were paid £50 a day for electric use and "inconvenience" but most hated the fact that every time the place was on the telly, it was for bad news. Oh what fun we used to have disrupting filming with slow walks through he set whilst they were filming.' (Kevin Holland)

'I guess it's all about shouting "NO MORE". Some people belittle the estate for TV adverts, or some other media ego trip that should never of been allowed to be broadcasted for so long. Such a bad stereotype against the nice gentle people who still live in the area.' (Danny Walters)

'I lived on the Missenden block it shows, where we were out Saturday mornings mopping our fronts with lemon and grapefruit washes. It was lovely, there was no washing hanging off the walkways. I had ten happy years on there, and never any trouble, best neighbours in the world.' (Cathie MacIver)

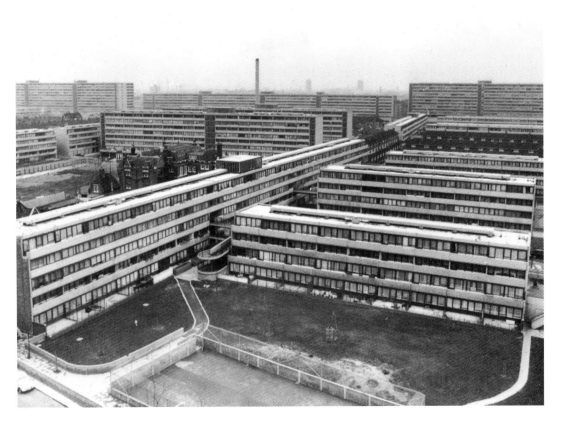

Drapers House

This was the tallest residential block of flats when it was built in 1965, It was named after The Drapers Co., who had almshouse in the area since the 1650s. The block has 133 apartments and stands twenty-five storeys high.

'My great aunt used to live on the top floor. I swear to God, that thing swayed on a windy day.' (Simon Richards)

'I think they were built to sway, not right over though.' (Tim Gillingwater)

'Running on the stairs, from top to bottom, was my exercise regime years ago. I even ran back up the stairs a few times! The things we did to entertain ourselves in the old days before laptops and computers.' (Tony McHale)

'We used to get chased out of there by the caretaker, when we were kids. We only went up there to look at the view.' (Colin Taylor)

'I used to hold the master keys to the roofs of all the blocks in SE17 and a few in SE5 & SE1. The views from the Draper House roof could not be beat. Especially amazing at sunset in June. The people below looked like ants. And as for fireworks night…' (Kevin Holland)

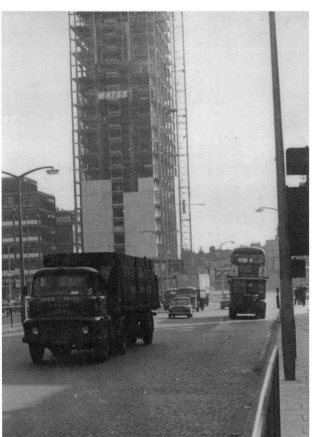

'It was the tallest residential block in London when it was built; I don't think it is listed but as Southwark have spent, so far, over £5M on the current refurb, it should be safe for a little while yet.' (Mark Brady)

'As my Dad was the caretaker, our family were the first to move into Draper House, number 5 on the second floor. We used to go up through the Pineapple pub as the entrance wasn't finished.' (Jo Clements)

'What a eye-sore.' (Jean Yeo)

Heygate Estate

A vast housing estate completed in 1974. In 2010, nearly all existing residents had been moved and rehoused, as a massive regeneration of the area began taking shape. Despite a 'bad press', many who lived there fondly remember it. There appears to be a lack of affordable social housing now being built on the new scheme, which has left many feeling angry.

'I don't like it – the regeneration – it's so sad.'(Neil Howie Aylward)

'Feel sad as I have great memories growing up there, but it needed to be changed. I feel sorry for the older people that can't move away or choose where they got rehoused. Luckily my mum and dad got somewhere nice.' (Shahia Greer)

'Before they moved us out, those that didn't want to move were told at least fifty per cent of the new estate would be flats for social housing and that we'd have first choice to move back. Don't look like that now.' (Mandy Olliffe)

'It is shameful what is happening there, apparently only seventeen of the new properties will be for social rent, the rest are for sale or shared ownership, with price tags of 1.5 million downwards, something not quite right about that.' (Kevin McCarthy)

'Who apart from Chinese investors can afford to live there? The local people haven't got a hope of affording a place here.' (Alan Davies)

'I remember it going up, all new and posh. Funny how all the old London County Council flats have outlived the Heygate, eh?' (Maggie Webb)

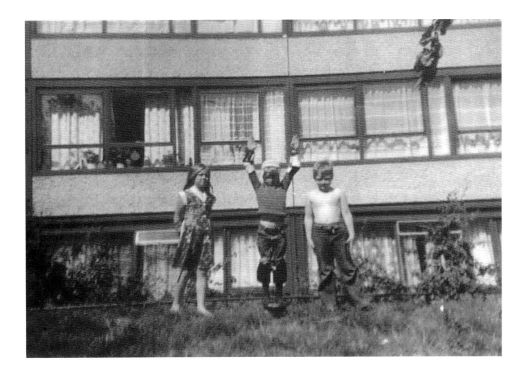

Brandon Estate

One of the first high-rise developments in London built in the late '50s/early '60s. It was named after Thomas Brandon, an eighteenth-century land developer in the Walworth area.

'They didn't get a great deal wrong with the Brandon Estate, and yet ten years later they got a lot wrong with the Aylesbury and The Heygate.' (Jacko McInroy)

'We lived in Penrose Street facing The Beehive pub and loved going to the Brandon Club Bingo Club and its dances.' (Ellen Tabrett)

'I remember using the Brandon library so often, then going home to Doddington Grove and playing libraries with my mates!' (Valerie Moseley)

'I lived on the Brandon from 1960 until 1990. A great community spirit existed in the '60s and '70s. I have some fantastic memories of the place from those days.' (Don Rougvie)

'I lived at 12 Farmers Road and witnessed all my friends and their families being moved out to make way for the Brandon to be built. Though they were delighted to get inside toilets and running hot water. I had loads of friends on the Brandon Estate because my mum and dad's house was left standing for quite a few years after it was finished.' (Janithia)

'I grew up on the Brandon Estate and I remember eating chips from Dandy's and frequenting the adventure playground, the swings and the paddling pool in the '70s and '80s.' (Donna Howard)

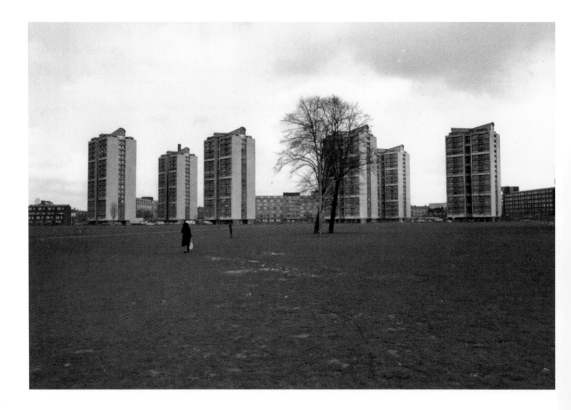

Manor Place Shops

A little area that is fondly remembered for the shops that were there. Among them was a barbers, a furniture shop, a dairy and the newsagent run by Mr Morrish.

'Remember those shops on Manor Place, down the Braganza Street end? Mr. Morrish and his sweet shop was a great favourite for us kids living in Doddington Grove.' (Alan Barrett)

'My dad Terry and my uncle Jimmy McGinley had a shop there called T. J. Furnishings.' (Terry Evans)

'Great memories and especially of the dairy and Pete's Barbers. Does anyone know what happened to Pete? I used to get my hair cut there up until three or four years ago when he just disappeared?' (Terry Wadman)

'I always remember Pete cutting my hair how he wanted to do it. Never what my mum asked for. Used to see him standing outside his shop and even giving me a quick trim for free.' (James Lynch)

'My father-in-law Les Morrish and his son, my husband Chris lived and worked there along with Harry and Win.' (Linda Morrish)

'I remember the firework club there, and his own made lollies, 1*d*, 2*d*, 3*d* and the ice cream.' (John Townsend)

'My dad was a milkman at Morgan's Dairy and I used to get a Corgi car every Friday from him. He used to have my own catalogue in the shop.' (Keith Stead)

'I bought my pea shooter and peas there.' (Billy Mason)

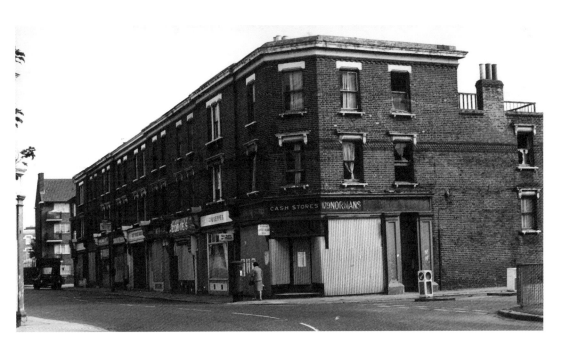

Saltwood Grove

Part of the housing scheme initiated by Octavia Hill (1838–1912), a well-respected social reformer, who campaigned for affordable housing in inner London. This housing stock is behind St Peter's church, off Liverpool Grove.

'My family lived at number 15 when we were young and then I ended up there again at number 36 in 1987 in my first ever flat. Loved it around there. It's between Liverpool Grove and Merrow Street.' (Neil Watson)

'My cousin Joyce Hill lived at number 26 and I remember watching the 1953 Cup Final on her TV. It was as big as a chest of drawers with a nine-inch screen. Does anyone remember Fred, the disabled old boy? He used a three-wheeled wheelchair that he propelled with a hand driven bicycle mechanism. It was probably late '50s.' (Richard Mann)

'Yes Richard, he lived under us in Saltwood Grove. I was very young and terrified of him. He was a nasty spiteful old devil and did some awful things.' (Kathy Porch)

'I lived at number 10 for most of my life and my Nan and grandad before us. My mum was born in the flat too. Good memories.' (Louise Goldswain)

'We lived at number 14 in late '76, early '77. Number 14 was haunted then, and the people who moved in after we left, tracked us down a few years after and asked us if we had seen anything strange? They then told us exactly the same occurrences our family had experienced. Then they won the Pools!' (Aerron Eales)

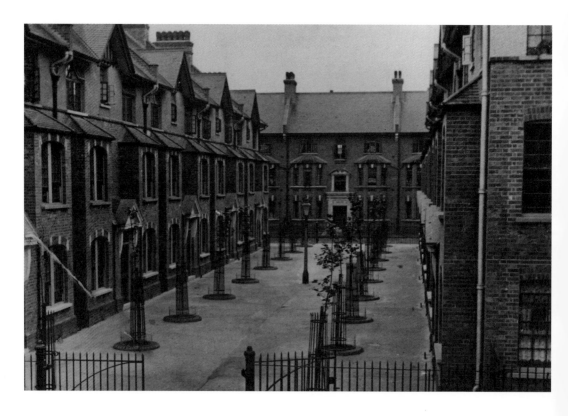

Chapter Four

There Are Faces I Remember

Nicky Clarke

Hairstylist to royalty and celebs from all over the globe, Nicky Clarke was born and raised just off the Old Kent Road. He was apprenticed to Leonard of Mayfair where he learnt his trade, subsequently opening his own salon in the same area in 1991.

'Nicky is my dad's cousin. He comes out of Madron Street, just of The Old Kent Road, near to Kinglake Street.' (Warren Lake)

'I think Nicky's first salon was on the Old Kent Road?' (Christine Simpson)

'His dad worked at the Bankside Power Station, which is now Tate Modern. Very smartly dressed man he was. I read later he had his suits made on Savile Row.' (Dave Sainsbury)

'I am a cousin of Nicky Clarke. My dad and his dad are brothers. Aunt Rena, Nicky's Mum was 90 in April 2013.' (Jennie Trotter)

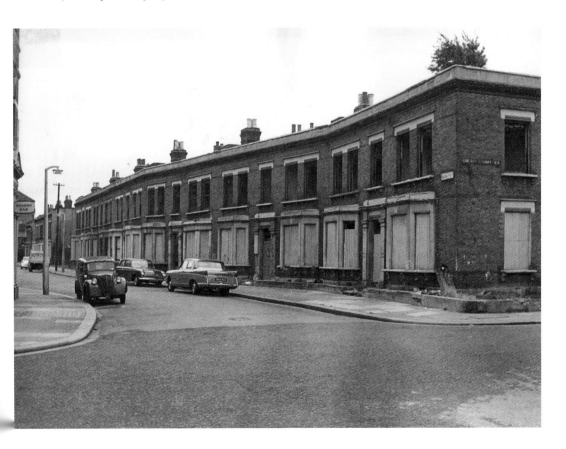

Henry Cooper, 1934–2011

Born in Lambeth, 'Our Enry' was a familiar face in and around Walworth in the early 1960s, due to him training at the gym above The Thomas A Becket pub on the Old Kent Road. He ended up a British, Commonwealth and European heavyweight champion, though he is best remembered for knocking down Cassius Clay (later Muhammad Ali) in a fight at Wembley in 1963.

'I met Henry and his promoter Jack Solomon at "Toby's Club" in 1965, nice man.' (Glenn Fiander)

'Henry used to have his suits made to measure. I was 14 and did basic tailoring for Sydney Rose on the Old Kent Road in my school holidays. I felt so privileged to have delivered Henry's big broad jacket to the Becket for him to pick up wear.' (Brian Tanner)

'Cooper fought Clay/Ali twice and the fights were at Wembley first (non-title) and Highbury. The controversial moment came at the end of the fourth round in the first fight, when Clay's trainer clearly breached the rules. In the second fight Cooper was always second best. Henry never did fight in the US, but he did fight at Manor place though!' (Mark Brady)

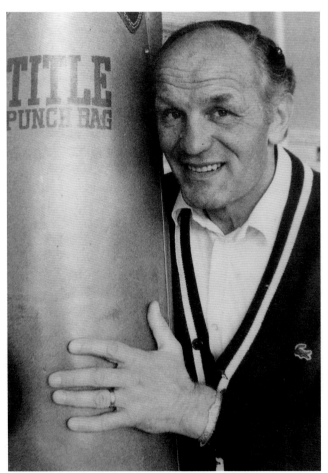

'I remember an interview with Clay/Ali, who said Henry hit him the hardest ever. When Cooper was asked what was the hardest he had been hit, he told a story about driving accidently into a cyclist. He went to help up this little weedy bloke from the wreckage of his bicycle and the bloke was so angry that he smacked Henry one and floored him.' (Jim Cutler)

'I was there on the night of the Bugner fight. Ten of us went that night, and nine out of 10 marked Bugner the winner. None of us could believe what we'd done because we all wanted Henry to win. All these years later, take away the sentiment, and I hate saying it, but Bugner ended with the most points.' (Mick Collins)

Doctor John Crane

A much loved local GP and well-known face in the area of Walworth, Dr Crane was also the team doctor for Arsenal football club for over thirty years, and also filled the same role for the England national team. For the last years of his working life, his practice was at No. 70 Camberwell Road. He died in early 2009. A John Crane Street in SE17 was named in his honour in early 2014.

'He was our doctor and he had a chalet on the Isle of Sheppey. We also had a caravan down there and would spend the whole six week summer holidays there. One year my brother Ross got run over on Portland Street, and Dr Crane arranged with my mum to take my brother to his chalet to have his check-up so we didn't have to return to London! An amazing doctor. I couldn't imagine a GP doing that these days!' (Alison Handford Martins)

'Dr Crane was our family Dr and he literally saved my life in 1972. Saw him and spoke to him a few times briefly in 2001 when hubby and I were following England footy team round the country. When England were at Old Trafford – the day before the famous England *vs.* Greece World Cup game in October 2001 – he gave me his England cap. We swapped addresses. I was so sad to hear he passed away. Dr Crane impressed my Mum, and that took some doing back in the old days!' (Kay Alexander)

'Best doctor ever. My Nan had cancer and she was fed that she couldn't get off the settee. When he came up for his daily visit and we told him she was fed up, he went straight into the front room to her and scooped her up in his arms and took her in the kitchen and then walked up and down with her in his arms about ten times. He then went back to the front room and plonked her down. I said careful and he said "don't worry about her she's tough as old boots!" My Nan was cracking up, she loved it.' (Sharon Hannah)

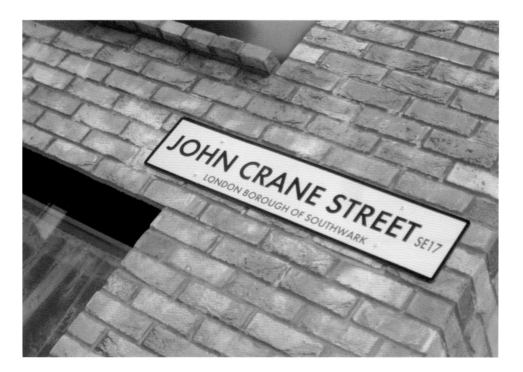

Fred 'Nosher' Powell

Born in nearby Camberwell in 1928, Nosher was a very familiar face on British TV in the 1960s and '70s and worked as a stuntman on more than one hundred films and television series. He was also a minder for J. Paul Getty and Sammy Davis Jnr., and sparring partner for boxers Joe Louis and Muhammad Ali, and worked as door security in his later life.

'I remember seeing him in Foxes, the jean store as a kid in the 70's down the top of East Street market.' (Tony Thumwood)

'I got to know Nosher when I started working the doors. He gave me a good insight into the job, which I did for 25 years. A legend.' (Roger D'andrade)

'My dad Charlie Waite worked with him in the Fruit Market (Covent Garden) for many years.' (Suzanne Penhall)

'My mother-in-law said he was a wonderful dancer, and just after the war he used to have a queue of girls lining up to "cut a rug" with him!' (Christine Martin)

'Nosher was my great-grandmother's nephew, his mother was Lillian Powell and his father Fred Powell who was my grandmother's brother. His father was one of eleven children of which only five made it to old age. His father's family was originally wealthy fairground people, who later ran fish and veg stalls in East Lane market. Nosher was a great character, larger than life.' (Carley Talbot)

'My mum and dad were very good friends with him. There was a story of going to a party at his mum's house in the early '50s. My sister had just been born and they took her up there in a pram. When the pram wouldn't get through the front door, mum and dad were about to go home when Nosher came running down the street after them, holding the street door that he'd just taken off its hinges so they could get the pram in! What a man.' (Barry Brewer)

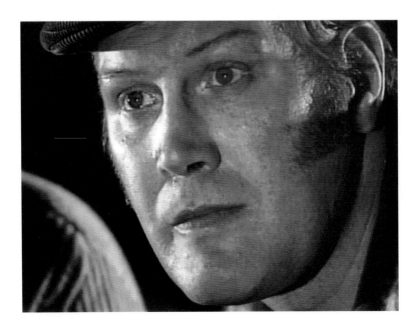

Harry Cole

Harry was a local 'bobby on the beat' stationed at Carter Street, Walworth for over thirty years. After his retirement, he became a well-known author and his books were very popular with residents of SE17. He was awarded the British Empire Medal in 1978 and died in 2008.

'I read all of Harry Cole's books, about when he was a policeman. They're so funny. I could sit and read them again now as it happens. I might get a set off on Amazon.' (Irene Jacobs Kebell)

'He was still there in the '70s and he dealt with me a couple of times as a pre-teen. Helped point me in the right direction.' (Tony McHale)

'*Policeman's Progress* is a very good book. I read them all over 20 years ago. All good reading.' (George Lowe)

'I've got all of Harry Cole's books. They remind me of the Walworth I use to know.' (Pat Morris)

'Shame he died, he was our local beat bobby and a true gentleman. I met him often as a kid and then much later at WHSmiths in about 1980, when he did a book signing session for *Policeman's Progress*.' (Don Rougvie)

'He used to see us across Camberwell New Road when we were going to school at Comber Grove.' (Eileen Cook Vines)

'I once asked him if he could see me across the street. At that, he ran across to the other side of the road and shouted: "if you're the little fat bloke with the glasses, then yes."'I thought – cheek!' (Jacko McInroy)

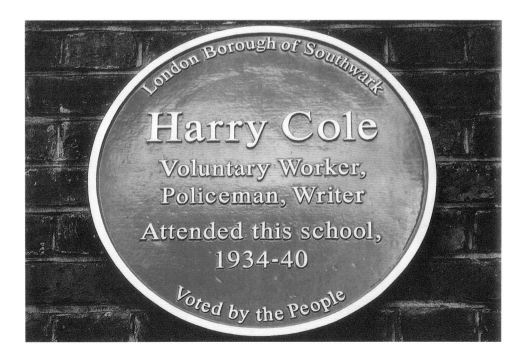

Charlie Drake, 'Hello My Darlings!'

Best known as a comedian and singer, Charles Edward Springall (Drake was his mother's maiden name) was born in 1925 and died in 2006. He was born at the Elephant and Castle and lived in and around Walworth for many years.

'I believe he was born in Delverton Road, near Manor Place.' (Dorothy McEvoy)

'My Nan used to clean for his Mum.' (Linda Wales Callahan)

'My mum dated Charlie Drake when she was young and she worked in the NAAFI in Kennington, before she met my dad. It's a standing joke in our family, as my youngest brother Georgie looks suspiciously like him!' (Nicky Wentworth)

'I went to see Charlie Drake at the London Palladium in *The Man in the Moon*. I remember getting the black cab from the Walworth Road and wearing our Sunday best.' (Marian Pearce)

'He lived in Draper House at the Elephant for donkeys years, rented I believe, even when he was very famous.' (Betty Lyons)

'When I was a nipper, I remember Charlie's nephew Tim lived in Deacon Street, and when Charlie visited he took all the local kids to the sweet shop in his rolls Royce and got us sweets.' (Alan Davies)

'I worked with Charlie's sister, at WHSmith, in Elephant & Castle.' (Fred Davey)

'Loved him, saw him years ago at a pantomime at the Lewisham Theatre, so funny.' (Janet Allford)

'I remember the Charlie Drake show on the telly, he would greet Mr Pugh with "Morning Mr Poo".' (Pat Pagligara)

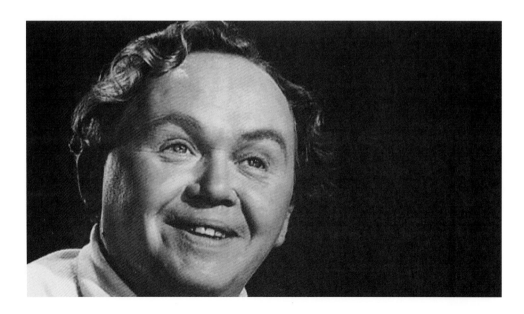

Lloyd Honeyghan – World Champion Boxer

A one-time resident of the Heygate Estate, Lloyd caused a major upset when he beat Don Curry for the Welterweight belt in America in 1986. Nicknamed 'the Ragamuffin', Honeyghan finished his career in 1995. He is still a frequent visitor to the area of SE17 and is always warmly received.

'I think remember he won the world title and came back to the estate and all the kids were chasing him. He went to Snowfields primary school, same as David Haye.' (Terry Evans)

'Didn't he come up the Walworth Road in an open top bus?' (Wendy Rodgers Pocknell)

'I was there amongst that crowd, brought back memories. All down the Walworth Road and into the Old Kent Road. He stopped off at the 'Beckett' where Dennie Mancini his corner man, held up the number 7 round card to the open top bus. I got a touch of the WBC belt on Dunton Bridge. I can remember waking up so early to watch the news for the result. Nobody gave him a chance against the Lone Star Cobra, as Curry was known, who, at the time, was ranked the best pound for pound fighter in the world. I couldn't believe my eyes watching the news!' (Darren Chandler)

'He went to Paragon and he was in my class 'till I moved out of Walworth. He was a nice fella, good for a laugh.' (Colin Taylor)

'Top top bloke. Knocking Don Curry out as he did, awesome man. Heygate's finest. Massive supporter of kids' boxing. Helped me no end when when I was rounding up all the little "ragamuffins". Respect.' (Kevin Holland)

'My Mum made the sparkly boxing shorts he wore. She was asked by the tailors on the Walworth Road.' (Lucy Christofi Patriotis)

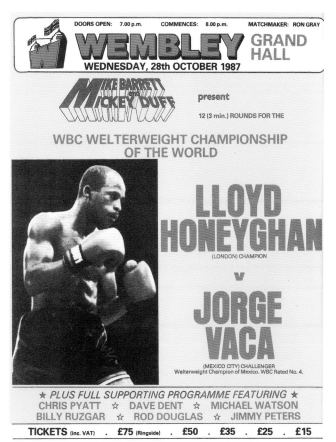

Lisa Maxwell – Actress and Television Presenter
Born in Elephant and Castle in 1963, she is best known for her role as Samantha Nixon in the ITV drama *The Bill,* and as a main panelist on the show *Loose Women.*

'Lisa lived in Rockingham Street.' (Jill Macey Browning)

'On the Rockingham?' (Jill Jolly)

'Yes, she did. I've read her autobiography *Not That Kinda Girl.* A good read.' (Christine Waters)

'I lived next door to Lisa, No. 37, when she was about 5. Knew her Nan well.' (Maureen Stanford)

'She also lived Draco Street next to my granddad.' (Bianca Brenland)

'True, my dad used to drink with her nan, granddad and mum in the Duke of Sutherland. Lisa came in occasionally. She used to drive a white Golf convertible with personal plate.' (Steve Judd)

'Lisa went to Joseph Lancaster School and she came from the Rockingham. Her cousins lived in Penton Place. I last saw her a couple of years back at a funeral.' (Mark Brady)

'Just about to read Lisa Maxwell's autobiography and the Duke of Clarence pub in Manor Place is mentioned in the first sentence.' (Dawn Worth)

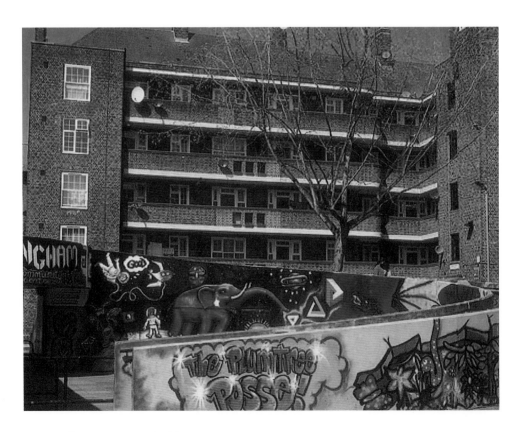

Michael Caine

Born Maurice Micklewhite in nearby Rotherhithe in 1933, he spent his teenage years in and around Camberwell and Elephant and Castle. His first acting work was undertaken at Clubland, a fondly remembered youth club run by Dr Jimmy Butterworth. He was knighted in the year 2000, returning to the area for the 2009 film *Harry Brown*, which was set on the Heygate Estate.

'I've always loved Michael Caine; after all he went to my primary school – John Ruskin. In his biography, whilst recalling the hardship and poverty of his youth, he also recognises the spirit of the people. In all interviews I have seen, he never hides from his humble values.' (Don Rougvie)

'I also went to John Ruskin Primary, and later, Wilson's Grammar School in Camberwell, where Michael Caine also attended, although I believe he was not very happy there.' (Ted Jones)

'I lived in Urlwin Street and Michael Caine lived at number 13.' (Irene Benson)

'I have been told "Clubland'''is where Michael Caine did his first performance.' (Mark Taylor)

'He did used to go to "Clubland", which is almost opposite Albany Road. Once I had a dance with him. He had beautiful eyes. He is a few years older than me, but I'll never forget that dance.' (Maureen Doe)

'I saw the film *Harry Brown*, starring Michael Cane, on Sunday. That film was made on the Heygate.' (Pauline Gill)

'When he filmed *Harry Brown* there were constant references to Caine returning to his East End roots. They got that wrong. They even mentioned how he kept a flat nearby. His flat is actually in Chelsea Harbour!' (Jackie Wallace)

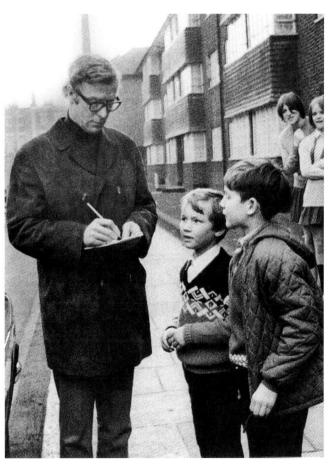

Kenny Sansom – Born in 1958

Kenny is fondly remembered locally as probably the best footballer to come from the area. He played 172 times for Crystal Palace, 314 times for Arsenal and 86 times for England. He retired in 1994 and has since suffered with alcohol and gambling issues, and is currently in treatment for those. Both authors wish him well.

'Brandon FC featuring Kenny Sansom. A crew from Westcott nicked our bonfire one year, so me and Kenny bunked off school and nicked it back, plank for plank!' (Patricia Durant)

'My Dad, Joe Wilson, set up that team, and he had a few players in that team that made it professionally, Kenny being one of them. Dad was a scout at Millwall for over twenty-five years and only retired a few years ago!' (Jacqui Taylor)

'I used to live in the same block as Kenny and his family in John Ruskin Street, such a lovely family.' (Mandy Hayler)

'I was in the same class at Beaufoy School with Kenny for 5 years, '70–'75 ish.' (Keith Bone)

'I had one date with him back in the days when his sister Mary was my sister-in-law's mate. I went on the date to make my boyfriend jealous; it worked, we later married! At the time Kenny was in the England Under-21 England team and at Crystal Palace.' (Irene O'Brien)

'He used to come and coach the Heygate footy team between 1973 and 1975, when he was visiting his family on the Cuddington.' (Tony Williams)

'I met him once and he told me his first date with his wife was at the Wimpy in the Walworth Road and they later married at St Peters. When he played for Arsenal he used to have his pie and mash delivered from Arments because Roy was a big fan.' (Darren Lock)

'And I did the disco at his wedding!' (Brian Watson)

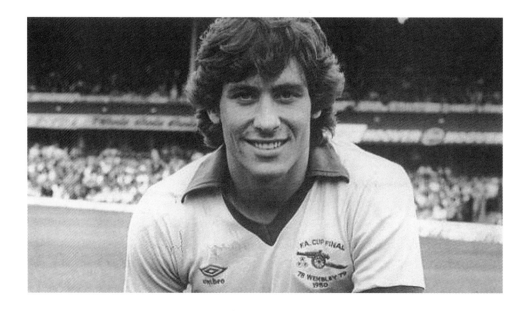

Chapter Five

Hatch 'em. Match 'em and Despatch 'em.

Edland Wedding, 1940s, St Peter's Church
A local wedding with quite a lot of bridesmaids.

'Look at all the bridesmaids, how many is it, six?' (Irene Jacobs-Kebell)

'Seven. Hold on, could be eight? Eight girls with flowers on their heads…' (Steve Langton)

'It is eight. All my mum's sisters. The one in the darker dress, is my mum's twin.' (Maggie Webb)

'Oh it is! What a lovely wedding.' (Irene Jacobs-Kebell)

'Why do women get excited by weddings?' (Steve Langton)

'Because they know what's coming. Rolling pinned hubby under the thumb! Only joking ladies.' (Maurice Haben)

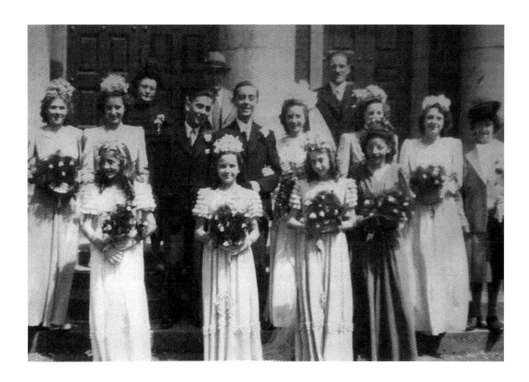

The Wedding Tree

A local landmark with many memories. It is situated in a park between St Peter's church and St Peter's School.

'I love this tree! I always went to the park with my nan, over sixty years ago. Love the willow.' (Margaret Bradford)

'We used to have picnics under that tree.' (Pauline Taylor)

'The tree of many names. We called it 'The Picnic Tree', some kids called it 'The Wishing Tree', that's going back to the '50s. Ahh, so nice to see it still there.' (Maggie Webb)

'I had my first kiss under there ha ha.' (Carla Hazel)

'We called this "the Witches Tree", and the hut was where she lived.' (Denise Sneath)

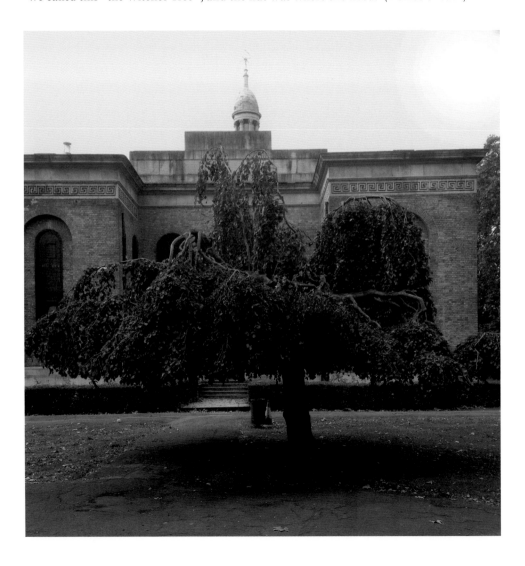

The Black Cat Caterers

Once a restaurant that began trading in the 1880s, it was perhaps better known as a local catering firm, who seemingly took care of every wedding in the SE17 in the 1950s/1960s. As the advert says, it used to be on the site of No. 240 Walworth Road, before moving to Camberwell Green.

'They moved from Walworth Road to the parade of shops in Camberwell Road opp. the Nags Head pub around the mid/late '70s. They were next to the shop that sold Airfix models and Scaletrix.' (Mark Brady)

'I catered for all my daughters' wedding parties from the Black Cat. All four of 'em! We got all the plates from there, tablecloths, platters … really good value and a good service. Can't fault, could do with one of them today.' (Betty Nicholson)

'Got my Chopper bike from Edwardes the bike shop next door or so from there. Dark purple it was. Six years later, went back and booked my wedding reception at Black Cat!' (Sheils Elaines)

'I got married in 1964, and the cost was £90 for around 80/90 guests.' (Jenny Goodman)

'They did ours in 1964 12*s* 6*d* a head!' (William Davey)

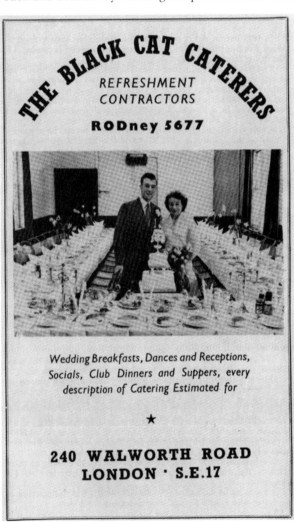

THE BLACK CAT CATERERS

REFRESHMENT CONTRACTORS

RODney 5677

Wedding Breakfasts, Dances and Receptions, Socials, Club Dinners and Suppers, every description of Catering Estimated for

★

240 WALWORTH ROAD LONDON · S.E.17

St John's Church/School, Larcom Street

A fondly remembered church, school and institute club in Larcom Street. It was very much the centre of Walworth life for many generations, something that continues today.

'I walked up and down that street four times a day to and from school. Only lived just around the corner so used to play down there too, unless the big Labrador that I was scared of was out!' (Jackie Tolfree)

'My old school. I was there between '53 and '59. The times I have walked down Charleston Street. What a lovely little church.' (Maggie Webb)

'I had Mr Ainsworth as head when I was there in the early '60s. Separate playgrounds and outside loos!' (Jan Stemp)

The institute used to get a fair bit of use. Monday night – youth club, Tuesday and Wednesday – cubs. Servers use to go in there on Thursday after practice. There were dance classes too, the bingo, school dinners during the day. The bar at weekends. Hope it's still getting used!' (Jason Tomlins)

'When we were brownies in the '50s, we used to go to the beautiful little chapel at the top of the building. We also had our school dinners there too from St John's School and they had a clinic there too. I remember when I was about 7 going there on my own with a pain in my wrist and they painted purple stuff on it. I would tell the other schoolchildren to go if they had anything wrong with them to get painted too. My mum got a note from the clinic asking me not to keep doing it ha ha.' (Jenny Goodman)

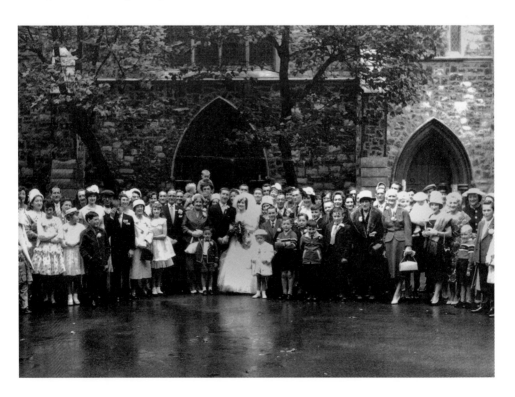

St Paul's Church, Lorrimore Square
The 1974 wedding of Patricia and Tony Goff. The Revd David Gerrard presides over the event.

'I was christened there in 1966, I remember it. I was four years old and done the same time as my younger brother, I think it was cheaper having two done at the same time bit, like happy hour!' (Bob Dobbs)

'My brother and I used to help at the weddings in the '60s. We used to get half a crown a wedding and we also played the bells, which then was a little piano. You had to play every other key to make the sound of bells.' (Elaine Wilson)

'My sister was married there too about the same time, mid-1970s, my mum paid for the bells to be rung. We thought they played a tape recording of church bells. We thought that was poor, so thanks for clearing up that mystery after all these years.' (Barrie and Janice Gilliam)

'My cousin and me would carry candles for Sunday service and some weddings in mid-1970s. Then go downstairs to play table tennis after.' (Nick Dear)

'I got married there on 22 August 1977 by the same vicar. I was also christened there 56 years ago!' (Lorraine Pendry)

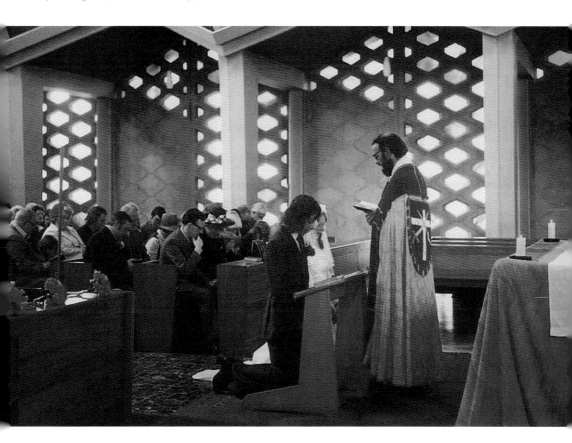

Communion at English Martyrs Church Courtyard
English Martyrs church was founded in 1890, and the Carmelite community here was established in 1980. The area provides a few challenges, being one of the largest housing estates in Europe, but it also enjoys a richness and vibrancy that comes from the multi-ethnic nature of the community.

The photograph below shows the first communion of Antonella Provini and her sister, Patricia.

'You're going to love this Patsy. This is me and my sister Patricia with our beloved mum and dad. That's Bridie, Irene Ray's mum behind Patsy and us and her mum in front.' (Antonella Provini)

'Oh My God! How cute do we look? How time flies.' (Patsy Murray)

'My Dad used to take me to Peckham, to Our Lady of Sorrows Church, to watch the procession when the children had their first communion. My granddaughter's was much different – no procession throughout the streets!' (Patricia Dinley Davis)

'I later went to St Veronicas with most of the girls from English Martyrs. I live in Hampshire now but come to Walworth a lot to see family.' (Sharon Roberts)

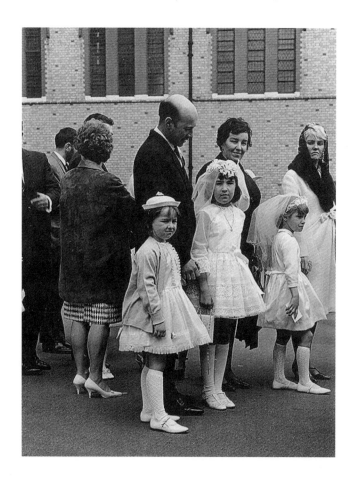

Funerals

What would you take with you on that last journey from Walworth?

'Been chatting with a friend today whose husband passed away recently. In his coffin, she will place a pack of Refresher sweets, his favourites, and she also told me of a friend who was buried with an empty carrier bag, as no matter where she went she had one with her. Got me thinking about weird and wonderful things people must have been laid to rest with.' (Lisa Colquhoun)

'I work in a funeral directors, and there's not much you can't take with you. Never been shocked yet!' (Christine Hawkins)

'My old man went with his match ticket from the 1995 FA Cup replay between Arsenal and Millwall, which The Lions won 2-0. He was never happier at football, than on that night.' (Mark Baxter)

'When we buried my lovely nan, she had chocolate éclairs in with, her bags of them, plus her knitting and letters.' (Patricia Gaskin)

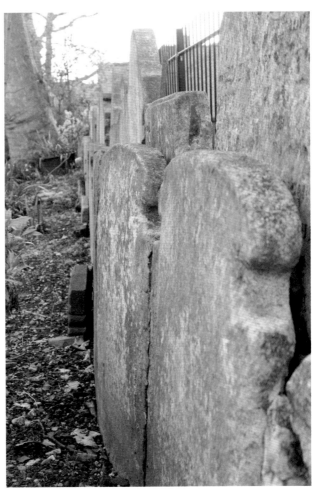

'My Mum's ashes went in the Thames, followed by her glasses so as she could see where she was going!' (Dawn Grifiths)

'My dad liked a bet, so I put a betting slip and one of those little pens they give you and he wore his cap as he always did when he went to put a bet on.' (Linda Grossmith)

'My dad was dressed in his suit and shoes and had a cigar put in he's top pocket.' (Denise Read)

'My dad had his trusty walking stick and a fiver in his hand.' (Susan Phillips)

'I want a fully charged mobile phone ... just in case!' (Pauline Curran)

A. Smiths, Funeral Directors

A local firm who has been taking care of the funerals of local SE17 people for many years. The original owner Alfred Smith sounds quite the character and fathered twenty-one children in and around the late 1880s. The company still has a shop under The Gateway on the Walworth Road, so that work continues in Walworth to this day.

'I work for Alfred Smith. The original Alf Smith had 21 children and when one died he was not over impressed so he asked a local businessman to teach him the trade and in 1881 the business was born. The business is still owned and run by family members.' (Christine Hawkins)

'Our family funeral directors.' (Linda Collingwood)

'From the mid '70s to the '90s, I booked the funerals for St Philip's, St Anselms and St Mary's parish churches in Kennington with Smith's. Then they looked after the family and me when my husband John sadly died in 2008.' (Bet Nicholson)

'Peter there looked after us when my mum dad died. All my family had Smiths.' (Jackie Barratt)

'Did my dad's funeral in 1950 and then went on to do quite a few family members.' (Sue Ives)

'Alf Smith had his yard in Newington Crescent and he used to drink in The Giraffe with my dad. If Alf was short of staff my dad would step in – this was back in the late '50s. He kept his horses in that yard, then he went over to Rolls Royce.' (Bernie Bowbrick)

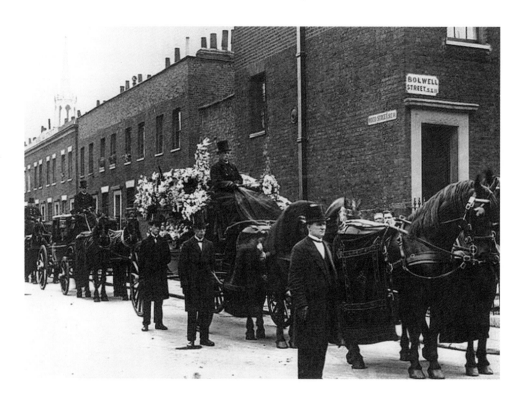

The Crypt at St Peters Church

Designed by Sir John Soane, the church has been at the centre of many lives in Walworth since building work began in 1823. Its crypt has also been used for a variety of functions over the years and that continues today, with bingo, sewing clubs and now a brand new café, run by Louisa Smith, also of the nearby Electric Elephant café.

'I used to go to the youth club here twice a week and a regular disco; it was such a great place.' (Susan Territt)

'The crypt was used as a youth club and in later years it opened the bar.' (Chrissie Brown)

'I used to get severely drunk there on Sunday lunchtimes. Always seemed a strange way for a church to carry on!' (Brian Whatley)

'There was always a lot of talk about strange things happening down there. If my memory serves me right, the beer delivery drivers refused to go in there and would only drop at the door after seeing a figure walking about.' (Neil Watson)

'There was a great youth club run by Mr Hutt, the school caretaker. We learnt to ballroom dance there and play snooker, and I always remember my first bottle of coke and the crisps with the salt in a little bag!' (Rita Drake)

'It's wonderful to see how they've developed the crypt. During the '50s and '60s, the youth club was in the church hall in Villa Street, on the site of the current vicarage. Betty Simpson ran it and heating came from a large coke fuelled potbelly stove. In those days only a small part of the crypt was utilised as a storage space for odds and ends, including trestle tables and chairs, which were used for fetes and fairs on, what is now, the ornamental garden. I've popped into the crypt for lunch on a couple of occasions and its excellent.' (Richard Mann)

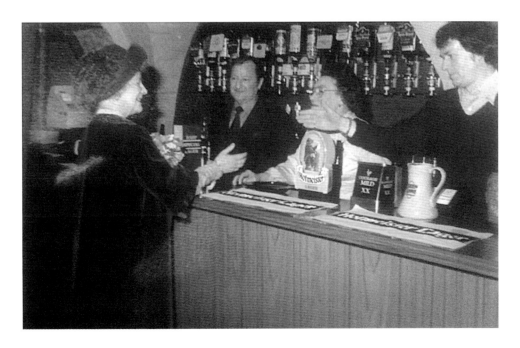

Chapter Six

This Sporting Life

Manor Place Boxing Nights – Manor Place Baths, Early 1970s
It used to be said that there was only a few ways out of the poverty of the area in the 'old days' – boxing, singing or becoming a criminal. Well, many chose boxing, and this great photograph is at the end of a bout at Manor Place Baths, which was normally a swimming pool that was boarded over for boxing bouts.

'The bruises on their faces are bigger that the cup, bless 'em.' (Louise Nicholson)

'That's George Cottle, next to well-known commentator Harry Carpenter. Another thorough gentleman.' (Tracey Charlesworth-Smith)

'I used to watch my fiend Phil Peru box here and my cousin Tony Earl boxed here too. I stuck to the swimming, far safer!' (Robbie Earl)

'Is that Bobby Paget in the denim jacket? He used to work for Frank Warren.' (Les Allen)

'I knew Bobby Paget and his wife, Sheila, great friends of mine. Me and my mum and dad lived in Kettleby House and they lived in the block opposite.' (Margaret Leahy)

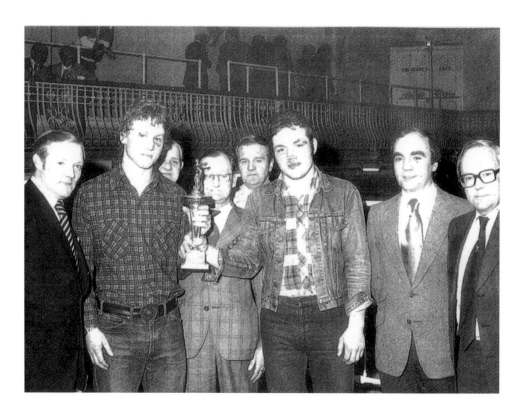

The 1966 World Cup Final

The finals that year were played in England and the national team, led by Bobby Moore, were victorious in the final *vs*. West Germany on 30 July, winning 4-2 after extra time, with striker Geoff Hurst scoring a hat-trick.

'On July 28th, the Thursday I gave birth to a daughter, I was promised I could go home next day but because she was born at nearly midnight they wouldn't let me out until Saturday, World Cup day. I thought my husband would have a nervous breakdown waiting for the Doctor to release me, finally let me go at 1.30 p.m. The one good thing was I had a girl, if it was a boy he wanted to call it Willie, after World Cup Willie, the mascot that year.' (Joan Herbert)

'I was coming up for ten and remember going to the toilet during the match, surrounded by blocks of flats. Whilst sitting having a wee, England scored and it frightened the life out of me, because of the sound of people cheering!' (Gill Masters)

'I was driving a 184 bus up Denmark Hill when we scored our first goal. I think the bus must have gone all over the road!' (Bernie Bowbrick)

'My sister got married that day. Saw the first half at home and listened to second half in the church on my radio with an ear piece, and watched extra time at the British Relay shop on Walworth Road. What a reception we had in Penrose Hall that night.' (John Cordrey)

'I listened to it on the wireless at a stall down the Lane. Shouts from one end of it to the other when we won. They must have heard us in Berlin.' (Danny Crawley)

'On that day East Lane was alive. It was amazing – everyone dancing and singing, all the pubs were brilliant. We ended up that night in Trafalgar Square. Fantastic memories, I was 19 years old.' (Raynor Simpson)

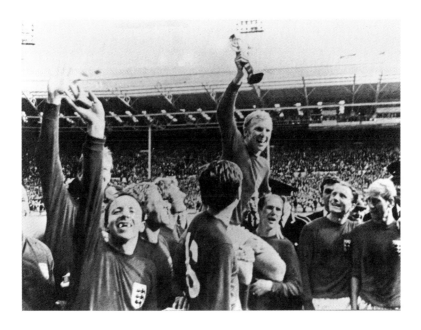

Darts in Pubs

A much-loved pastime of many in the Walworth area, there were hundreds of dart matches all over SE17, on any given week night. Each pub had a team and there would be friendly rivalry among them all. In recent years, the game has become a TV sensation, with thousands in attendance for the World Championship each December.

'My great granddad, Henry Daniel Fletcher, on a day out for The Crown darts team in 1932. He's second from the left, stood up with an overcoat.' (Zoe Elizabeth Nelson)

'The Huntsman and Hounds had good darts teams. I played Darts in here.' (Karen Pooke)

'The pub has about 5 darts teams, and I'm in the Monday league and I'm very proud to be a part of it.' (Linda Burgess)

'My uncle passed away in there about 30 years ago. A special darts trophy was made in his memory. Would love to know what happened to it? His name was George Ling.' (Sue Lia)

'I remember the darts trophy Sue. It had his red darts placed in it. It was always on a shelf above the dartboard in the late '80s, early '90s.' (Darren Collingridge)

'I wish I had been the one selling those caps!' (Robert Callaghan)

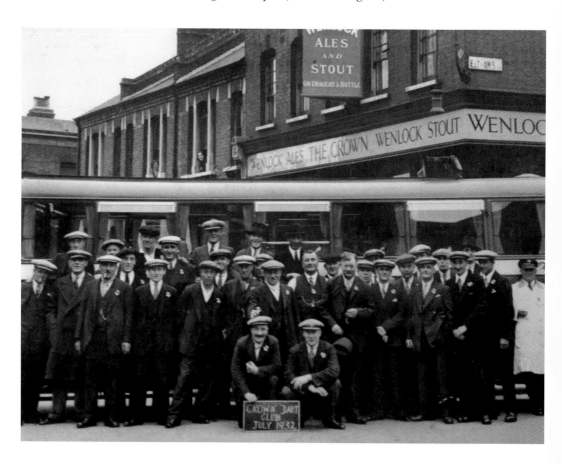

Football

Once memorably described by Chelsea and England player Alan Hudson as 'ballet dancing for the working classes', football has been by far the most popular sport to be played by boys over the years. Whether it was in the playground at break time or after school in the local park, there is always a game on somewhere. But who did the locals of SE17 actually support?

'I supported Chelsea as well, mainly because I liked Peter Osgood, nothing to do with the football ha ha! I think quite a few kids bunked of school to see the parade when Chelsea won the FA Cup in 1970.' (Kate Tarpey)

'If you were a true South Londoner from around Old Kent Road, you had to be Millwall!' (Peter Kenward)

'Always been an Arsenal fan, a gooner, as my brothers support them, but when we used to talk to people in the pub and they asked us why we came 'so far' – to North London where they played – I used to say that Arsenal were originally from South East London – they were originally from Woolwich!' (Julie Boon)

'I used to stand on the terraces at West Ham, Millwall, Chelsea, QPR, Charlton, Arsenal, Spurs and Palace – basically wherever we thought was the best game on that day. I come from Kennington, but I am a West Ham supporter. Most of all, I am a football fan!' (Lewis Waite)

'I remember seeing Corinthian Casuals play at The Oval, which they used as their home ground in the 1950s. I think Doug Insole was on the wing. He was an Essex batsman, and later chairman of the England cricket selectors. Lovely colours – Chocolate and Pink.' (Richard Mann)

'If you're from Walworth you have to support Millwall. It's the law!' (Frank Notton)

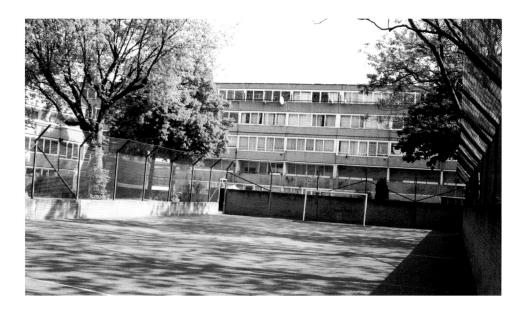

John Bennett Sports Shop

Founded in 1821, the company behind the name was well known for the high quality of their snooker tables. The shop settled on the Old Kent Road in the late 1960s and did a roaring trade in all manner of sporting goods. It closed in the mid-1980s.

'John Bennett's shop used to have a full sized snooker table presented in the shop window.' (Joe Power)

'Even though I was born in Guys hospital and went to Paragon School, and my dad always took me to watch Millwall, the first football kit I bought from John Bennett's was a Wolverhampton Wanderers one! I came to my senses though and bought a West Ham kit the following year!' (Allan Cooper)

'I remember they used to sell table tennis tables. Who used to buy them?' (Justin Bridle)

'I got my first swimming costume from Bennett's. Our school insisted on plain navy blue and it was the only place you could get them, as it was 1970 and everywhere else had psychedelic patterned ones!' (Patricia McGuigan)

'"The" place to go for Subbuteo!' (David Dennington)

'Remember it well, used to go upstairs and nick my Subbuteo teams ha!' (Keith Pheby)

'I worked in there from 1970 to 1984 and probably sold most of you your sports equipment. I won six awards for my window displays, and had to attend to over 60 break-ins. I was also lucky to meet a lot of the snooker stars at that time.' (Fred Davey)

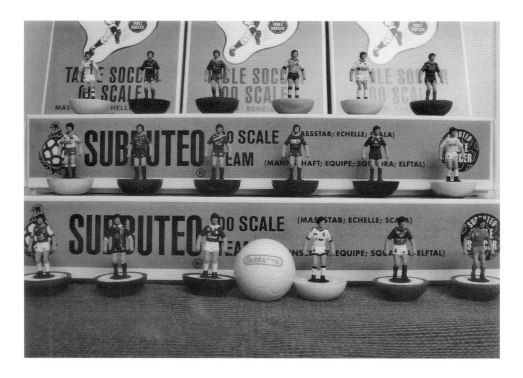

Swimming at Manor Place Baths

A Grade II listed building built in 1898, where generations of youngsters learned to swim in its three pools. It closed in 1978, replaced by the leisure centre at Elephant and Castle, which itself has now closed.

'You got a right crowd there! Everybody got thrown in the deep end whether they could swim or not, and if you swam too close to the diving boards you would be bombed. Still went every week though.' (Robert Callaghan)

'I remember buying bread and dripping here for one penny a slice after a swim.' (Roger The Dodger)

'I loved swimming here and getting a bag of chips wrapped in newspaper on way home.' (Caroline Ryan)

'I remember the three pools. The "small", the "second"(which was the same size) and the "first", which was my favourite. They used to have chalkboards outside on the window when it was busy telling you how long until next lot was allowed in. Great memories.' (Crispin Hudd)

'Learnt to swim there with John Ruskin School, and I still remember the broom handle just in front of my nose to grab on to if I got tired.' (Janice Eastman)

'The "first" pool had a balcony and they would cover it up for functions, boxing and that. Great memories.' (Tony Hill)

'Kids now spend £40 on a rucksack to carry their swim gear – we used to put ours in a rolled up towel and carry it under our arm, I still do. Always brings back good memories.' (Janice Gilliam)

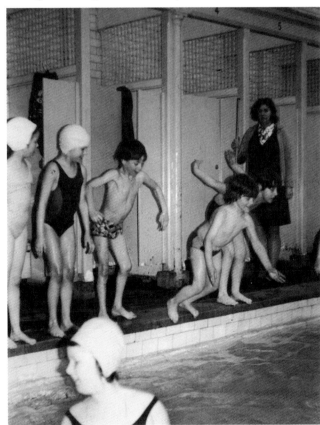

Burgess Park Lake

Part of a vast 13-acre site that started to take shape in the late 1960s, the park recently underwent a complete renovation. The lake is still a popular spot for the fisherman of the area.

'My Dad was a park keeper there for a while, and he remembers someone putting pike in it and they ate everything on site.' (Daniel Faulkner)

'My friends catch some big fish out of there, 20 pound plus. The first time I went fishing was at Burgess in 1986.' (Mark Whitton)

'We used to go "night fishing" there until the police caught us, ha!' (Jamie Colquhoun)

'I spent many days there with my then boyfriend fishing. Wish I could say what lovely memories they were, but I just remember being cold and bored.' (Samantha Collins)

'My mate "Peg Leg Terry" got pushed in and got his fishing gear nicked!' (Tony Peto)

'I can remember going on the boats over at the lake.' (Michelle Leigh Brosnan)

'I remember swimming in the lake and getting a slap when I got home from my mum. I was always thrown in the lake as well, my mum got fed up washing the clothes. I loved it!' (Nazamin Caffrey)

'My husband's first job was as a lifeguard at Burgess Park lake, from 1982, for several years. We lived in Chiltern in Aylesbury then.' (Bernice Dickenson)

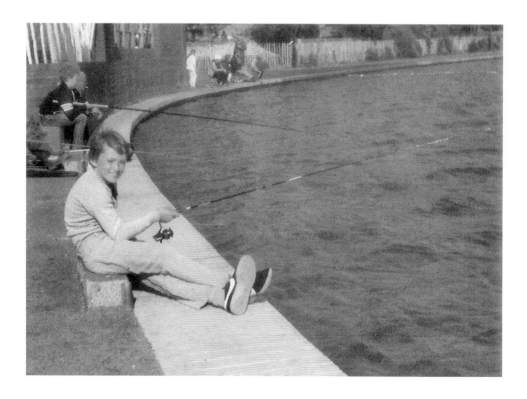

BMX Track – Burgess Park
Opened in August 2013, this track is the home of the Peckham BMX Club, run by CK Flash and his team of volunteers. The track cost in excess of a £1 million, but with BMX now an Olympic sport, perhaps a future gold medalist might come from the South East London area.

'I drove past there today it looks really good.' (Celina Medi)

'About time they put something in for the older kids.' (Liz Kielak)

'A couple of kids from the club that run this have made it into the British squad. Better they are out competing like this, than at each other in gang related nonsense – got to be a good thing surely?' (Dave Sainsbury)

'We have one near to where we live, it's used all the time and keeps the kids out of trouble and helps to keep them slim and fit.' (Les Allen)

'There's going to be sessions for younger kids and I read somewhere that there'll be sessions for adults too! The new way to embarrass your teenagers is to get a BMX. See you down there!' (Zara Lloyd)

'I have been over there on a Sunday morning and seen teams racing each other. It looks great and they come from all over London. A success for me.' (Catherine Nicholson)

'I was in Burgess Park today and had a really great time. The work they have done on it in the last few years is amazing and well worth the money. I'm sure the BMX track is going to be just as much a success as the revamped lake, the hills, the children's park, the fountains by the café, the café itself in Chumleigh Gardens and the tennis courts.' (Jacko McInroy)

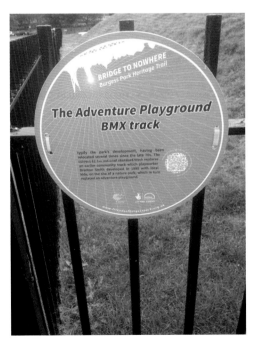
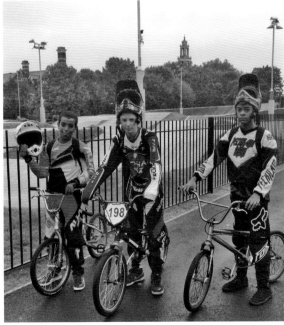

Betting

Betting has been a popular pastime for centuries. Following the Gaming Act of 1845, gambling in the UK was only allowed at racecourses. For those who couldn't get to a track, 'bookies' runners' operated on street corners illegally and took the wagers. This all changed in 1961 when the government legalised betting shops.

'I lived in Jesson House on Orb St between 1952 and 1963. My dad used to get me to go to a house at the other end of Elsted Street, and there was a man there who used to take bets. Never knew his name, but he disappeared if the police were around. Anyone else have to do the same thing?' (Sandra Brown)

'I remember the bookies' runners. One hid in my nan's outside loo once 'till the copper had passed!' (Maggie Webb)

'My granddad Fred lived in Beckway Street and he used to take bets I hear. He was also known as Darkie Morrell' (Shaun Meager)

'We lived in Doddington Grove, and almost every day in the early '50s I came home to dinner and on the way back to school I placed my dad's bet at a street bookie on the corner of Cooks Road and Lorrimore Road. Dad used to wrap the money inside a piece of paper with his bets written out. I would hand it over in the street and the man who took it slipped it into a big pocket inside his raincoat. Dad's codename was 'Tommy X', and if you had a win, you asked the man to settle and he gave you the winnings. One day I forgot to put his bet on and felt the money inside my pocket during the afternoon. I just prayed he hadn't won that day and told him I had forgotten after he had listened to the results on the wireless. I realised he had lost (as usual) and gave him his bet money back, saying sorry for forgetting. I still got shouted at but a backhanded compliment for being honest.' (Alan Bennett)

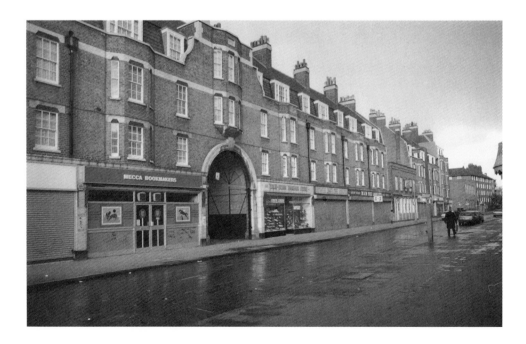

Chapter Seven
Shop 'Till Ya Drop

Bert's Fish and Chip Shop, SE17
We seem to always fondly remember our first fish and chip shop and Bert's is no exception, going by the comments below.

'I loved Bert's chip shop. My Nan and Granddad lived over the road in Congreve Street. I was always running over to get my chips, and then into Pat's sweet shop opposite and then Marie's, getting my Nan's ham and cheese cut with the old fashion cheese cutters.' (Vicki Peters)

'I used to always get sent down there on a Friday night when I was little to get fish and chips for me, my nan and granddad, Albert and Mary Chislett. They used to live right across the road from the shop. I also remember once going to Spain, and Bert and his family were on the same flight!' (Antony Fernandez)

'Suavely & chips and sit in the estate opposite on the wall.' (Keith Stead)

'This used to belong to one of my best school friends Maria. Her dad Bert always gave us a bit extra with our portions. Good times.' (Oz Eryeler)

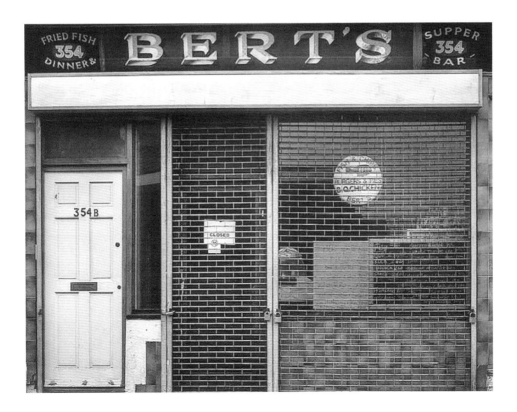

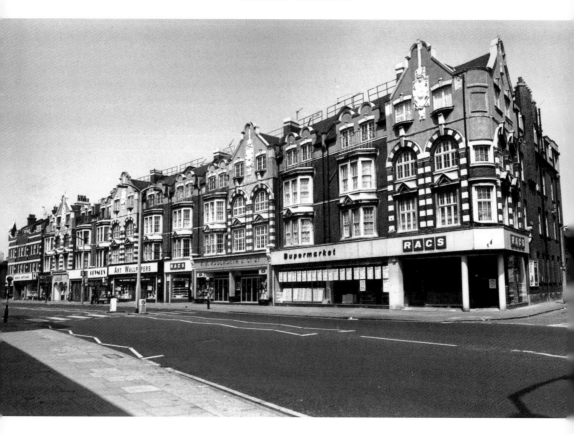

Woolworths

Founded in Liverpool in 1909, 'Woolies' was a familiar sight on every British high street, until it entered administration in 2009, resulting in the closure of its 807 stores and the loss of 27,00 jobs.

'Ah! Good old Woolworths, still miss it.' (Pat Maguire-Kybert)

'That's the wonder of Woolworths or Walworth.' (Danny Walters)

'I loved my Saturday job at Woolworths. I worked in the record department, stacked the food, and on the cheese counter. All day for £4.50, which I got in a little brown envelope. Used to go up to a little window and sign for it. I was only 14 when I started and you had to be 15 and three months to work there. So I had to leave, as I would have got them in trouble for underage working. Gutted at the time, such a laugh. Even used to go to the pub across the road at lunch times and then got a Chinese lunch from "Winners". Such good memories.' (Karen Pooke)

'I remember going in here with my mum after a trip down a East Lane, and she would buy me a quarter of brawn for my tea from the deli counter. I don't remember deli counters in any of the other Woolworth stores near us, just this one.' (Tricia Fitzpatrick)

'I sat on their steps when I was in slow labour with my daughter.' (Nicola Putman)

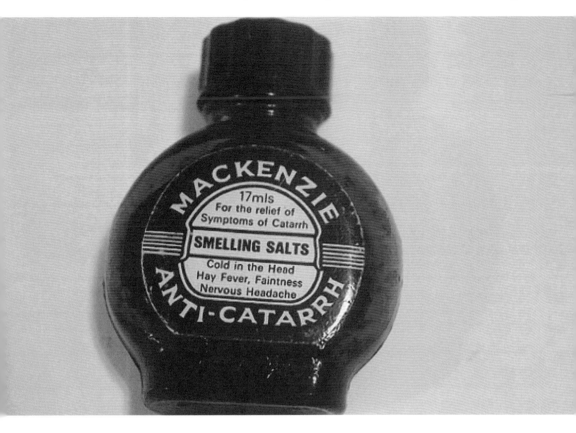

Briggs the Chemist, East Street

An independent chemist that became Knights in the early 1960s, and is still fondly remembered by the older generation of the area.

'Mr Knight, what a character! My old Nan used to tell him she wasn't well, "got a bad chest", and Mr Knight would knock something up himself, stick a label on it and people had no idea what it was. But trusted him, amazing days.' (Barrie and Janice Gillam)

'When I was very little, I fell over our fireguard and burnt one side of my face. My Mum pulled me out and rushed me up to Tommy Knight's, and he put something similar to Iodine on my face and informed my Mum she had done the right thing, as it would have been too late to get me to hospital. Every time he saw me even when I had grown up, he would say to people "look at his face you would never have known it had been burnt." Now the only time you might notice is when it's extremely cold it goes slightly purple. So I am very grateful to our chemist/doctor.' (Les Allen)

'I wonder if Tommy just knocked out the same "cure all" for all ailments? – Coughs, colds and runny 'oles!' (Valerie Bigsby)

Fred Harrison – Tailor, No. 45 Walworth Road, SE17
A well-established bespoke tailor. Fathers would take their sons to Fred's for their first work suit, a long-standing tradition. There is still a bespoke tailor on Walworth Road, operated by George Dyer at No. 187a.

'I had a wine coloured blazer made at Fred's in about 1960. It had silver buttons and a belt at the back. I had a badge on the pocket with my initials M.J.M. in italic writing. Topped off with Prince of Wales check strides. The shop was right near Levy's the tailors at the Elephant and Castle end of the Walworth Road. When they knocked the whole block down, Fred moved to the Cut, Waterloo way.' (Michael McClughen)

'I had my first suit made there with my mate Dave Sawyer. We thought we looked well tasty.' (Victor Wood)

'The telephone number sticks out on this receipt! Our phone number started off with HOP 407 and Rodney was 703. My dad went to Fred's.' (Lisa King)

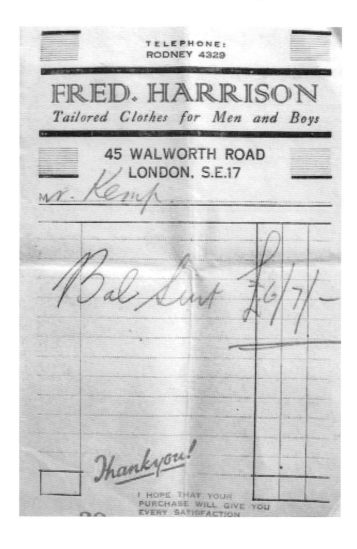

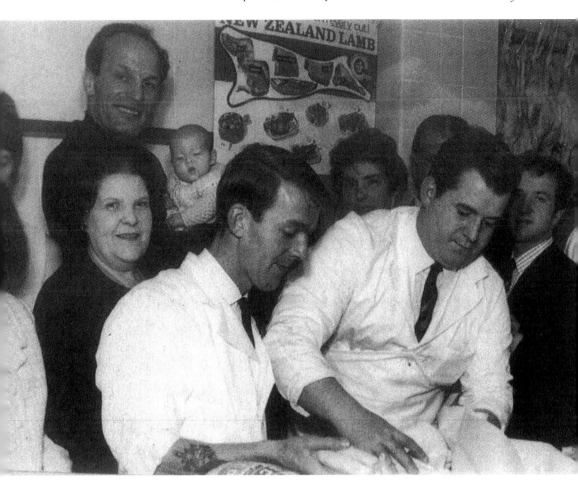

G. J. Petts – Quality Butchers, No. 5 Westmoreland Road, SE17
A local family butcher who has served the community for many years. Still open today, though sometimes only for a few hours a day, it is fondly thought of.

'I had completely forgotten this place. My mum was in there when she became ill and they had to call an ambulance for her, and it turned out she had an ulcer that had perforated. Funny how things like that are sent to the back of your mind!' (Don Bone)

'That shop was opened by the boxer Henry Cooper, who trained at The Thomas A Becket on the nearby Old Kent Road of course.' (Dave Sainsbury)

'Johnny Petts buys from our shop at Smithfield meat market. Nice old fella.' (Russell Raynsford)

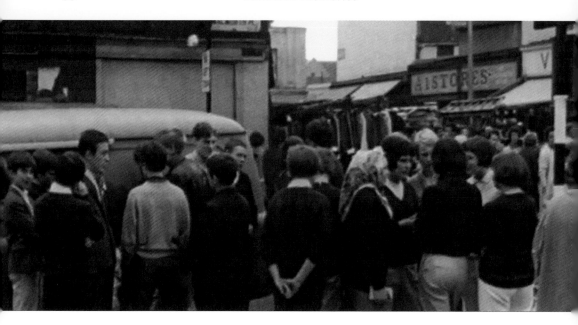

A1 Stores

This family run business opened in 1912. Over the years it also sold household lighting and greetings cards, but, for the majority of people, this is the place they bought that all important first single or album.

'My first record from A1 store, on the corner of East Street. It was by the group Sweet, only I can't remember the name of it? I used to go to the telephone box and ring up dial a disc as well and listen to the number one.' (Mandy Brace-Prescott)

'I too bought my first record there, Nat King Cole singing "Too Young", which makes me cry to this day. We never had a gramophone to play it on, so I would naively run a pin around it really fast! You guessed it, never worked!' (Suzanne Waite)

'I used to buy records in the A1 stores when we still had shillings and pence!' (Janet Grigg)

'I remember buying singles from the shop and the stall. I lived in Penrose Street, so every time I saved up a pound I would go and spend it there! Singles for six shillings and eight pence, in 1963, or three for a pound when my dad bought our new radiogram and I had my Dansette.' (Robbie Jackson)

'That sticker is on my copy of the 12" single of New Order's "Blue Monday", from 1983.' (Philip Shock)

British Relay Shop

British Relay was a forerunner to Sky Television. The service offered to subscribers meant, apart from better reception, an extra ITV regional channel and access to feature films.

'I remember when you put one shilling in the box and watched the films through a box on the floor. We then watched them for nothing at some point, I think it was a trial run in South East London which didn't last long.' (Marion Bassey)

'I remember we found a way of not paying, well, things were hard.' (Vivienne Pattenden)

'We had to put in half a crown to watch a film, but we put a bit of tissue in the slot and then pull out the shilling again.' (Jean Yeo)

'I remember that box, but ours was two shillings. We used to tap our one on its top with a hammer if it played up.' (Rita Beadle)

'It worked for four hours on French Francs.' (Terry Callaghan)

'I can remember watching the 1966 World Cup match as a kid on our small black-and-white British Relay telly. Great memories.' (Don Rougvie)

'I remember that just as the Germans scored the shilling went out of the meter!' (June Walker)

'We lived in Braganza Street and found if we turned it upside down, we got it free. Everyone fiddled them, hence they went skint!' (Johnny Bennett)

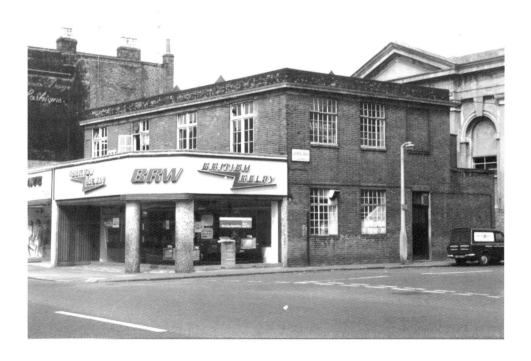

Arments, Pie and Mash

The shop celebrated 100 years of trading in 2014. This photograph from the family archive shows Emily Arment (background) and her father Mr Slater, taken above the shop where Emily, Peter and Bill Arment lived at No. 386 Walworth Road.

'My Mother worked in Arments 49 years ago, she was also Mr Arment's cleaner at his home in the Norwood.' (Robbie Earl)

'I was brought up on the stuff – it's what you know, and a taste of childhood. ARMENTS FOREVER!' (Rachel Collier Hines)

'In the mid 1950s, pie and mash was one shilling, you could get a thre'penny bowl too, just mash and liquor.' (Wendy Pocknell Rodgers)

'I moved away from Walworth in 1993, but have had pie and mash in Romford a couple of times when visiting friends, but not a patch on Arments.' (Susan Frampton)

'There are only three things you should put on pie and mash and that is 1. liquor, 2. vinegar and 3. pepper. Blimey, me mouth's watering!' (Sean Joyce)

'There is a whole generation out there that does not appreciate that liquor is parsley sauce. They are afraid to try it because it's green! Recently introduced some of my son's friends to the delights of pie, mash and liquor.' (Norah Skelton)

'Don't forget, a knife is the luxury item. They shouldn't be allowed to be used when eating it. Fork and spoon only!' (Lisa Stone)

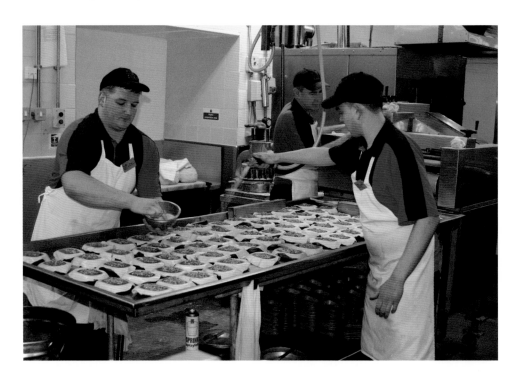

Bri-Line Cars

A much-loved mini cab office on Westmoreland Road. We believe everyone in the area used Bri-Line at least once in those years.

'Ronnie Ruddock owned Bri-Line. My Dad and him were best mates for many, many years. Ronnie and my dad not only worked in the box (control room) they also used to slip out and drive, when they weren't in the betting shop or round the pub playing cards. Ron had all the cab drivers driving about for my wedding in 1991 ... most of them, including Ronnie were at my wedding!' (Kim Filbee)

'Ronnie was best friend to my granddad. Lived a couple doors from me in Eugene Cotter House. I remember doing the cab cards for Ronnie, you know posting through letter boxes for sweet money, and I watched Lady Di's wedding from a chair in Bri-Line. Those were the days.' (Lynn Sells)

'My Dad was also a taxi driver at Bri-Line years and years ago. Anyone remember Dennis Logan?' (Danielle Logan)

'Bri-Line cab office can be seen in the video for the single "The Fly" by U2.' (Jacko McInroy)

'Heard old Ronnie died recently, real shame to hear, a real character and a nice man, funny too.' (Fred Harris)

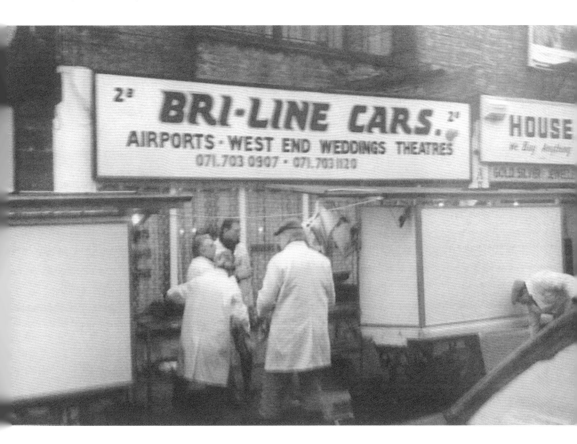

Taylor's Depository

A much loved shop that sold good-quality and ornate furniture and a room full of *objet d'art* – ornaments of every description. It appears that most flats or houses in Walworth had at least a piece of 'something' from Taylor's.

'I used to work in Taylor's. The man that owned it was called George Harrison and his mum used to run it. We called her Mrs H. Fred the manager.' (Brendan Walsh)

'George Harrison was big mates with Georgie Best and Bestie was often in one of the flats above the shop with a girlfriend or two.' ('Big Steve')

'My parents got loads of bits from Taylor's. Ornaments, lamps, a "what not" and a display cabinet.' (Louise Bee)

'I loved Taylor's. I still have a porcelain penguin in my living room that my brother bought in there for £75, about 25 years ago, and that was expensive then.' (Sharon Hackett)

'I remember Taylor's so well. I bought my beautiful cream bedroom suite at Waring and Gillow in Regent Street, and then was so pleased that Taylor's were selling copies of the same quality. I could then buy more of it.' (Suzanne Waite)

'I have a large cheetah ornament from Taylor's that my husband bought me over forty years ago, he's beautiful and people always ask where it came from. He cost £60 all that time ago and we call him Charlie, he's been through four house moves. If you felt a bit down it was the place to go and treat yourself to something nice, you could always find something there, a beautiful shop always with a lovely dressed window.' (Lia Lodge)

'My sister lived above Taylor's when her youngest was born and I got sent round to clean the flat. The floorboards collapsed and I wound up with my legs dangling in the shop!' (Diane Charlesworth)

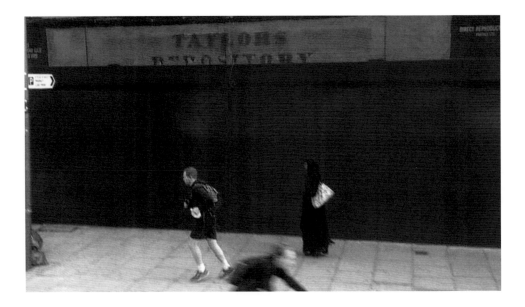

The Coal Man

A once familiar sight on the streets of SE17, when a coal fire was all most people had to keep their houses warm. Early housing estate flats also had coal bunkers and a coalman's horse, parked up, happily eating from his nose bag as children played football around him, was commonly seen.

'I remember the coal, man delivering to us. I think his name was Woods and from the Elephant he used a horse and cart. I thought he had two horses but it was a long time ago.' (Allen Transport Kilkeel)

'My granddad used to go round behind these with his little shovel and hand cart to collect the manure for his garden.' (Sue Ives)

'Oh, another memory – the coal man! The kids today wouldn't have a clue.' (Maggie Phipps)

'Coal marks up the stairs, on the walls, from the sacks when we lived on the first floor.' (Billy Mason)

'I loved the smell of the coal and would happily help shovel it into the coalbunker!' (Daryl Chandler)

'The coal man used to scare me!' (Sue Lavender)

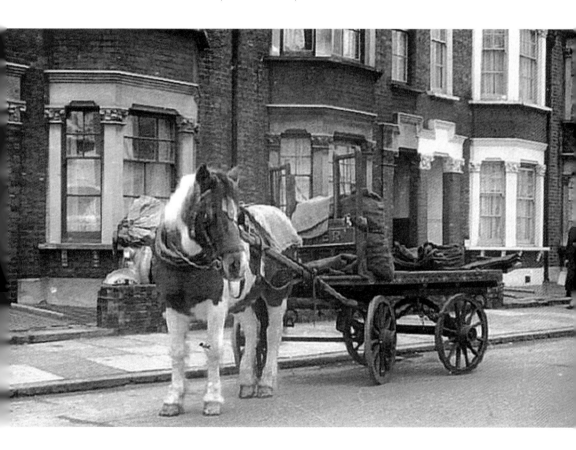

Half-Day Closing

The Shops Act of 1911 allowed for a half-day holiday during the week from 1.30 p.m. for shop staff. Wednesdays and Thursdays were a popular choice among many owners, something that is long gone and almost forgotten in light of today's 24-hour society.

'Who remembers half-day closing on a Thursday in Walworth? There was nowhere to buy anything. Wasn't it awful?' (Betty Lyons)

'I remember half-day closing well and you couldn't buy a birthday card on a Sunday because the shops were only allowed to sell certain items.' (Pam Good)

'Soap powder wasn't allowed to be sold on a Sunday.' (Kevin Mullins)

'Very few shops on the Walworth Road would be open on a Sunday, but those down East Lane would be mainly open, with a few exceptions. Under the old law you could not buy a bible on a Sunday, but you could buy a porno mag!' (Christine Simpson)

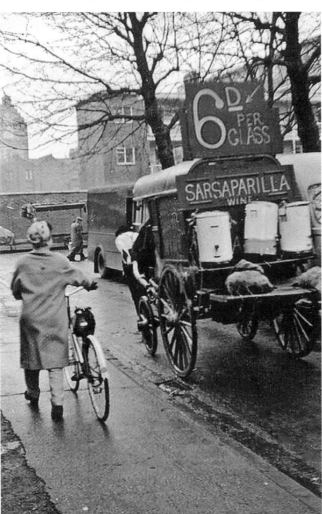

'My dad closed half day and then in the end it was all day, as half a day seemed a waste of time. He would never answer the phone in shop on Cup final day, the day of the grand national or on the Wimbledon finals day because people complained their TV was broken and he knew he wouldn't get it fixed in time.' (Malcolm Cowan)

'Remember when the pubs shut at 2 p.m. on a Sunday 'till 7 p.m? This got me into cricket as we went to the Oval cricket ground where the bar was open all day.' (Jonny Hawkes)

Chapter Eight

The Streets of SE17

Street Parties

A tradition that started in Britain in 1919 and named as 'Peace Teas' by the residents who set them after the signing of the Treaty of Versailles. They have continued for Coronation days, VE day, signaling the end of the Second World War, and the Queen's Jubilee ever since. An estimated 10 million people took part in the Silver Jubilee in 1977.

'Could be the George VI coronation of 1937? Some of the children are wearing pith-type helmets, but can't make out the writing on their front? It could read "The Coronation"?' (Len Sadler)

'That's Blackwood Street. At the other end of the photo is my Nan and Granddad with my dad and a couple of my aunts. Also I think Ada Rumble. We have a copy of this photo but taken from the other end of the table.' (Ann Pickering)

'All the ladies wore wrap-over aprons and the men caps in those days. I remember my nan and granddad always wore them.' (Maureen Doe)

'I lived in Frederick Road and remember a big street party marking end of World War Two. Later we went to Trafalgar Square and saw the grown-ups dancing everywhere!' (Mary Wrigley)

'As I remember it, there was a small Gilford's on the corner of Portland Street and Trafalgar Street. We used to stop there for a custard tart on the way down East Lane.' (Valerie Bigsby)

'There was a dairy on that corner and opposite there was a row of shops including Loll's sweetshop, Dr Weatherup's surgery and the paraffin shop.' (Rita Drake)

'I wonder if you can still get those aprons?' (Maria Sharp-Olliffe)

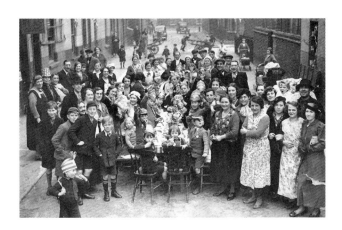

The Bag Wash

Before the widespread use of self-service launderettes in the early to mid-1960s, many people would use a 'bag wash' service, where each bag of clothes to be cleaned would be emptied into a machine and washed with a strong bleach-type cleaner, with no separation for colours. Each bag would be numbered so people got back the right clothes.

'My brother and me had to take ours to the bag wash in Westmoreland Road on our way to school at Michael Faraday. I remember the bag sat in the hall, and I used to step on it so I could reach to open the front door.' (Pauline Gill)

'We used to pin all the socks together, so as not to lose them!' (Brenda J. Powell)

'There used to be a number on the bag and it smelt a bit like bleach. We used to get mum's sheets back, all wrapped up in brown paper and string.' (Wendy Rodgers Pocknell)

'In the early '50s, you'd take in at nine in the morning a pick it up at four in the afternoon.' (Jean Yeo)

'I remember we used to take ours to a cleaners down "The Lane"'. Mum would throw it over the iron gate of the shop early on the way to work. Many a time something ran and we would all be wearing the same shade of underwear, all pink! Dad was not impressed!' (Tina Camp McCarthy)

'We used to take bag wash down "The Lane" and then hang it in the drying rooms in the flats. Good old days but hard at times. Never bored or lonely though.' (Ellen Clark Smeby)

'We used the one in Westmoreland Road in the '40s and '50s and then they opened the first launderette in Walworth Road.' (Barbara Nay)

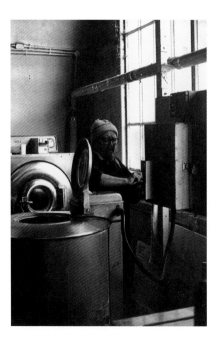
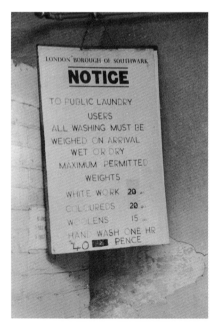

Bombsites

As a result of heavy bombing over South East London in the Second World War, a multitude of 'bomb sites' remained in situ well into the late '60s and early '70s, even later in some places. Of course, they soon became the playgrounds of the young in the area. Health and safety officers nowadays would shut them down immediately, but then they were different times...

'The potatoes we put in our fires were black outside and rock hard inside. I was all of seven or eight! We played out 'till dark in them days.' (Betty Lyons)

'It was a sort of initiation test, to be a street raker. None of your silver foil then. We stuck them on a stick and poked them in the fire. I can still remember the feel of gritty charred wood in my teeth! We did the same with big cooking apples one year. All our faces were twisted because they were so sour!' (Pauline Curran)

'My brother injured himself on the one in King and Queen Street. He was climbing on the wall, fell, and ripped his arm on the barbed wire and then fell onto a rust bedspring. He was nine, I still remember that day.' (Jackie Tolfree)

'We used to look for unexploded bombs when we was kids, good job we never found any!' (Chris Owen)

'I used to play on them all the time. Trying to find stuff – gas masks, shrapnel – anything really. I broke my arm when I fell through a floor one day. I told my mum that a gang had beat me up, as I wasn't allowed in the old houses. My sister went out looking for them! I didn't tell them for about thirty years. Great times.' (John Townsend)

'Ours was in a bombed house in Camberwell New Road. We used to roll newspaper and smoke it!' (Elaine Gorman)

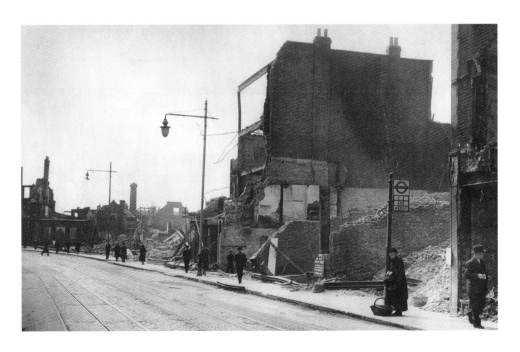

Bonfires

The name is derived from fires in which bones were burned, and the run up to the 5th of November was always a time of excitement. The younger ones would be out doing 'Penny For The Guy', trying to raise some funds to buy fireworks, while the older ones would be collecting any spare wood for the ever-growing bonfire, which was always built on the same patch of wasteland year after year. In these days of health and safety, displays have become organized and a lot safer, but that personal touch has been lost.

'Our bonfire was on St Agnes Place bombsite next to church. My mum had a rocket go up her coat when the milk bottle it was in, fell over!' (Jackie Mattingley)

'Our bomb fires were in Doddington Grove, right in the middle of the road. There used to be about four fires on the go – amazing.' (Margaret Bradford)

'We had ours at the end of Kinglake Street and Madron Street. You could feel the heat as you stepped out of your front door!' (Lynn Newlyn)

'Ours was on the corner of Rodney Road, opposite Youldings the butchers and English Martyrs Hall. There were always lots of armchairs and sofas to burn, and the old 'uns used to sit on them 'till they were needed for the fire, which was still smoldering when you went to school the next morning.' (William Davey)

'We did ours in my friend Janet's backyard and her mum made cheese straws and chips cooked in dripping. Yum.' (Betty Lyons)

'Ours was at the Merrow Street end of Saltwood Grove. Much of the timber came from the ruined buildings around Arnside and Lytham Street. Neighbours would pool their fireworks in a big tin bath. Thank God a spark didn't drop into that!' (Richard Mann)

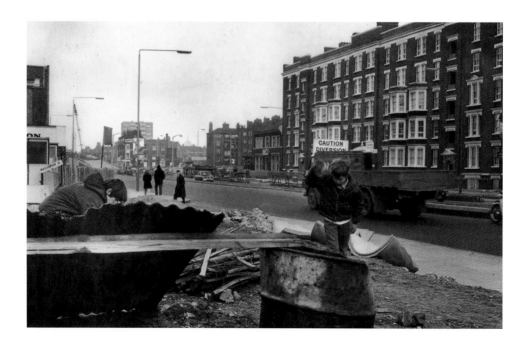

Air Raid

During the Second World War, the underground tunnels at the Elephant and Castle tube stations were used on a regular basis as shelters, during bombing raids by the Luftwaffe.

'My Mum used to tell me how people sheltered in the underground during the war.' (Barrie Gillam)

'When strangers became friends they helped each other out.' (Jacqui Lowry)

'I remember the day the Elephant and Castle opened. We all went to have a go on the moving stairs.' (Kay Clark)

'We slept there as kids and our mum also used the borough underground. We don't realise what people went through and we moan over such trivial things now, Ah well that's life.' (Josie Walker)

'When German bombs were falling on London the underground was the best place to be. Health and safety then? I don't think so. I'm just glad I was a post-war baby, born in 1948.' (John Cox)

'I remember being there with all my brothers and sisters and running to it with our mum, eight of us. It was terrific, but I was so frightened as I was only four years old. I remember it as if it was yesterday. Life was so tough. My poor mum.' (Kathleen Tomlin)

'I remember carrying a pillow and blanket with my mum and brother, they were bigger than us! We had our Mickey Mouse gas masks and we used to line up and the nurse used to give us a hot drink of milk. Looking back I think there was something in it to help us sleep. How my mum managed with all her kids evacuated out everywhere and just two little ones waiting to be evacuated with her, I'll never know. God Bless you Mum!' (Ellen Clark Smeby)

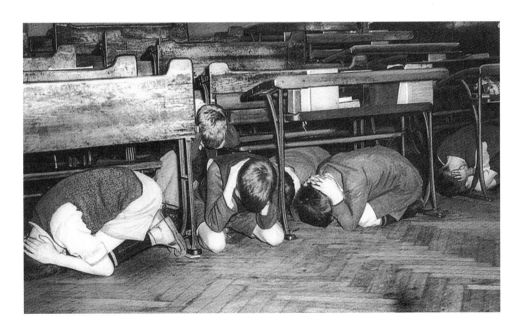

Games of the Street

Whereas many of today's children spend hours indoors playing computer games, the children after the Second World War up until a few years ago would make their own enjoyment in the streets, playing a succession of well remembered street games like 'Runouts', 'Knock Down Ginger', 'British Bulldog' and many others.

'Anyone fancy a game of "Runouts"?' (Danny Walters)

'Oh my God. I can hear my mum calling me in, ha ha.' (Jackie Barrett)

'I'm not playing anymore, anyway, that's the ice cream man music, MUM!!!' (Dean Chandler)

'I have always said that there should be playgrounds for adults only. I would love to run around and go on the swings and slides and seesaws etc. By the way, I am 60 going on 6.' (Janet Trent)

'What about a game of "Cannon"? Anyone remember that or hopscotch? You would not be allowed to chalk on the pavement nowadays, you would get a fine!' (Christine Sandra Dobbs)

'"Feign Lights!" Of course, when we were kids we would shout out "vein lights".' (Pauline Gill)

'Feign Lights! Wow, forgot about them! The council estate diplomatic immunity!' (Danny Walters)

'A friend and I were playing "Runouts" in Trevelyan House and we hid in one of those big smelly chute bins. We were there for ages, and then the doors opened and we thought we had been caught, but it was a lady there to empty her bins! We jumped up and shouted and she totally lost it and ran off screaming! Funny times!' (Lewis Waite)

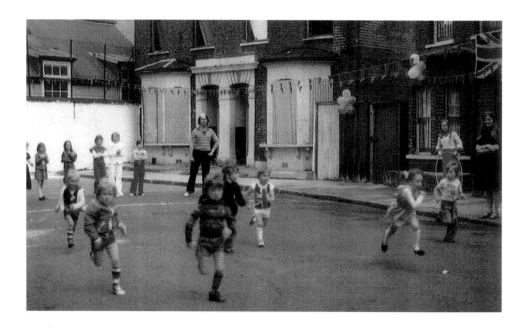

The Language of the Street

With the coming and going of generations of people in and out of SE17 over the years from all parts of the world, many of the old phrases once used in every day parlance are now seldom heard. But a rich history of street slang and sayings passed on over the years have resulted in some classic lines that are still fondly remembered; however, though many of the origins and meanings of the following are lost in the mists of time.

'My dad was not so popular with my grandparents. "Gawd, here comes Charlie Farnsbarnes" they'd say when he appeared.' (Peter Minter)

'You'll get a punch up the "weskit", often said my dear Nan.' (Emma Beesley)

'"Oi, noseache" to anyone who was nosey.' (Lee Summersby)

'When I was stressed and said to my Nana "what shall I do?" she'd say "Take off your stockings and pee in your shoe".' (Clare McCabe)

'My aunt Rose told me to "keep your hand and your ha' penny' whenever I was going out".' (Carole Bolton)

'"What's for tea mum?" "Air pie and windy pudding" came the reply.' (Patricia Wallis)

'I used to get told, "look where you are going, not where you've been".' (Jacqueline Seaward)

'Cough it up, it might be a gold watch.' (Richard Till)

'If my grandkids hurt themselves I say, "what are ya?", and they say with a laugh through their tears "a silly old kipper".' (Tina Camp McCarthy)

'If anyone farted my gran would say, "Catch that and I'll sew a button on it!" (Sandra Baker)

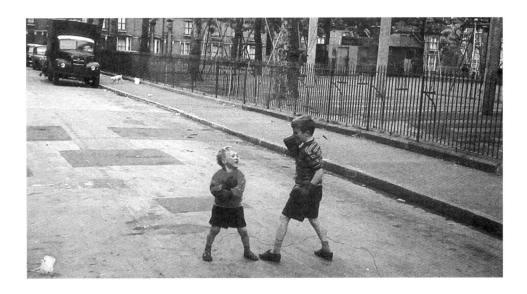

Phone Boxes

Before the days of mobile phones, there was a time when even having a telephone in your flat or house was unheard of by most of the working classes. The phone box in the street was where you had to go to make a call. Needless to say that over the years, many became vandalized or used for a ... different purpose.

'Ah the 2p calls, the paper phone directories and the stench of urine. Priceless!' (Tracey Mason)

'I spent hours listening to 160 Dial A Disc!' (Mandy Kelly)

'I remember when we got our first phone at home, I still had to go to a phone box to ring anyone because my dad wouldn't let me use the house one, said it cost too much!' (Sue Lia)

'I got pelted with snow one Christmas by in the Merrow Street phone box, ringing my mates up with my mug of tea, sitting on the phone books.' (Janice Tatham)

'You wouldn't spend long on the phone with the smell, or someone tapping on the window, or coughing, so you would hurry up.' (Maggie Kelly)

'I remember our first phone in Pilton Place. The number was "Rodney 8667", and mum developed a BBC telephone voice when she used it.' (Chris Owen)

'Haha! Yes my Mum developed a BBC voice too. If anyone asked for her, she would say "Yes, this is she".' (Pauline Gill)

'You used to get money back on using the A and B buttons in the old phone boxes. It was like hitting the jackpot when all the pennies used to come pouring out! Naughty I know, but we all did it.' (Shirley Bryant)

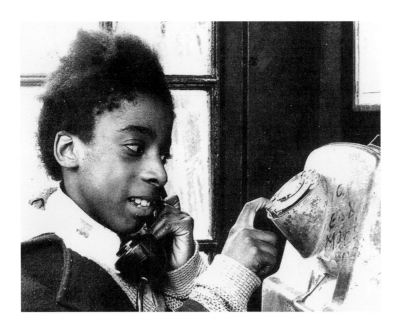

Chapter Nine

That's Entertainment

The Great Storm of 1987
This occurred during the night of the 15th and 16th of October. Gale-force winds caused severe damage to roads, buildings, parks and streets and resulted in power cuts in the Walworth and surrounding areas, as well as most of the UK. A certain BBC weatherman said on air that mentions of hurricane conditions were false alarms.

'The aftermath of the October storm of 1987, Forsyth Gardens. Some people's misfortune is another child's adventure playground.' (Nicky Wentworth)

'It was the 16th of October, which was my birthday, and we got the day off school!' (Lori Tink Townley-Parrott)

'I remember when that happened. Right outside my front door, wow!' (Katy Scriven)

'I slept through it and got up in the morning wondering why there was no electric? It was only when I went out to take my eldest to nursery, I realised why!' (Julie Thompson)

'I woke up to total darkness to find my old mum wandering around the flat with a candle, frightened the wassnames out of me.' (David Sainsbury)

'And that Michael Fish said nothing was going to happen didn't he? Always said the weathermen were liars. Liars the lot of 'em.' (Jean Baxter)

'My Mum used to tell me that thunder was God moving his furniture around!' (Kath Kenward-Jackson)

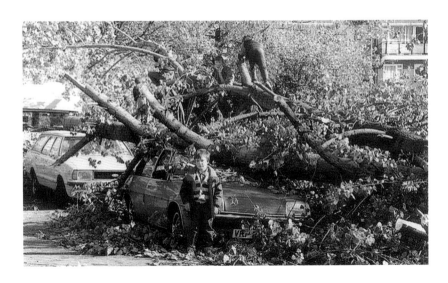

Clubland

Founded by the Revd Jimmy Butterworth, this youth club was opened in 1939 by Queen Mary. Among those who attended various functions there until its closure in 1977 were Bobby Kennedy, Bob Hope, Laurence Olivier and The Queen Mother. Today, it is home to a Methodist church.

'Opened by Queen Mary, widowed wife of George V and grandmother to Elizabeth.' (Robert Callaghan)

'What a great thing to of happened to Walworth, Clubland was something else. It created a safe, decent and influential environment for young people to flourish, development, and be positive people within society.' (Danny Walters)

'Brilliant place! I was in the drama group and loved it. It used to cost sixpence a time, and I played a judge in a production there. I also made a set of cushion covers for my nan, the first present I was ever able to give that I'd made and paid for myself. I was so proud of them.' (Carole Bolton)

'This was a great club, the first place I saw a stage show, which was *Oklahoma*. A great club for kids.' (Lia Lodge)

'When I went, probably 1953 or 1954, the boys and girls went in on different nights, only the older ones had dances some Saturday evenings. I was in Blue and was captain of Blue for a while.' (Valerie Bigsby)

'I remember Bob Hope coming. We attended the Sunday evening services too, only we missed one week and J. B., as Butterworth was known, noticed. "Did you enjoy the service?" he asked. "Yes" we said. Oh God, we were in trouble and banned for a week. He was a short man and had a temper, frightened the life out of me.' (Suzanne Waite)

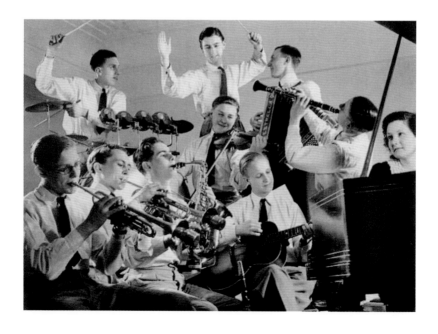

Terri Stevens

Born in 1952, Terri was well known on the Walworth Road pub circuit and later became famous after an appearance on the Simon Dee TV show *Dee Time* in early 1969. She later released records and appeared in West End shows. And touring in the USA. She was seen again recently on an episode of *The Voice* after a long sabbatical.

'Terri was a great singer. Sung in all the music pubs in the area, and did some singing in the USA.' (Les Allen)

'I used to live next door to her when I was little, when she was plain old Theresa Fogarty.' (Jacko McInroy)

'I went to school with her last time I saw her was in a London night club.' (Patricia Lillian Holton)

'She was fantastic, used to sing in the restaurant in Walworth Road. The Carousel? Had some great nights in there.' (Maggie Hughes)

'We were in the same class at John Ruskin (Mrs Letton's class) then both went to Trinity Girls' off the New Kent Road. She lived in the flats in Bethwin Road at primary school. Last time I saw her she was singing in the Temple Bar in the early seventies. Really good seeing her again on *The Voice* last night – brought back lots of memories from school days. Well done Teresa!' (Iris Schwartz)

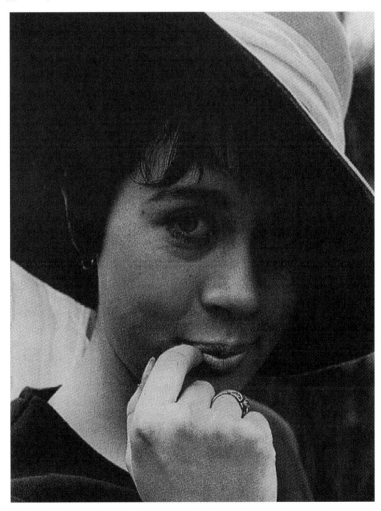

Tommy Cooper's Brother

One of the more bizarre sights on a Sunday down East Lane market was the brother of comedian and magician Tommy Cooper playing records from a stall. Us kids believed what we were told and that is who we thought it was. But now there is some dispute as to who he actually was? He looked very much like Tommy, with many of the same mannerisms, and again is well remembered.

'Remember the record stall down the "Lane" run by Tommy Cooper's brother? He sold the old 78s, think it was outside The Bell pub.' (Mark Taylor)

'I do, he stored his records in the shop I worked for at that time. The Cookery.' (Charlie Taylor)

'I've heard the "Tommy Cooper's brother" thing so many times, but nobody has been able to confirm it as true. What era was this? I know Tommy's brother David had a magic shop in Slough.' (Mark Brady)

'It was David definitely and he used to drink in the Bell.' (Alan Davies)

'We knew him as Harry Cooper and, as far as I know, he was indeed Tommy's brother. We sometimes had our stall next to his and I would be in stitches hearing his voice and comments.' (Jim Cutler)

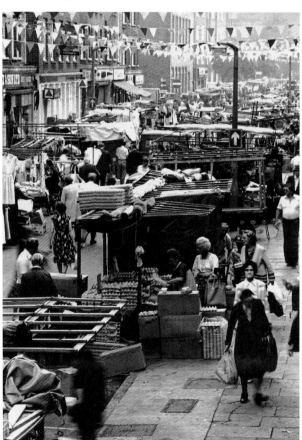

'He used to sing out the tunes! He had a rather funny looking assistant, they both used to wear old trench coats.' (Daryl Chandler)

'He also sold ex-juke box 45s with a big hole in the middle which had to be filled in with a plastic disc called a frog.' (Len Sadler)

I remember him well. Big lump he was, dancing about to the records he put on. Every time I went down there with me granddad in the late '70s, he'd say "see that man there? He's Tommy Cooper's brother." Never doubted it … 'till now.' (Dave Baxter)

The Frog and Nightgown

A well loved pub at the flyover end of the Old Kent Road. From my personal memory it had blacked out windows that gave it a foreboding appearance to outsiders. Dare they venture in? Plenty did and here are some of their tales.

'The Frog was my stepdad's local and I went there a couple of time myself. Smartest place in the Old Kent Road.' (Diana Saxelby)

'It was a very smart pub. I remember when it first opened, it was very modern then and that is where I met my husband. He used to DJ in there on a Wednesday – The "Varisound Disco".' (Janet Grigg)

'I remember Peters and Lee performing at the Frog.' (Ken Hampson)

'Superb pub, especially on a Monday afternoon. Anybody remember the band East End?' (Gordon Ford)

'I remember the Frog for the saucy ladies nights in mid-1980s. Now they were good!' (Jan Baker)

'My husband had his stag party there in 1985 and got so drunk, while in the loo, he nearly fell over, but grabbed a pipe to steady himself and brought down the toilet system!' (Ann Amor-Sheridan)

'I went to the Frog after one of my cousins got married, had a massive row with my other half and got the engagement ring chucked at me in East Street on the way home. Other than that had some great nights in there.' (Steve Casey)

'Read somewhere that it was fictitious name, which was used in a radio show from the '50s.' (Mark Brady)

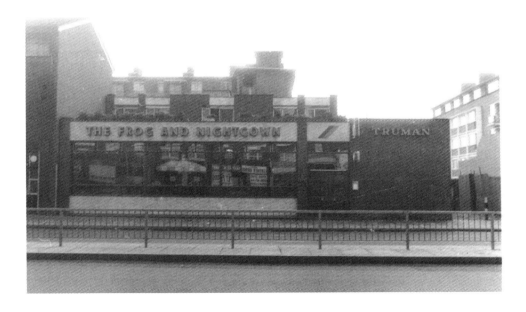

Nine Below Zero

A local band who went onto to attain national recognition and chart success. They were led by Walworth boy Dennis Greaves, and managed by local lad Mickey Modern, who has kindly contributed for this book. The band is still going strong and travel all over Europe and the UK.

'They were formerly called Stan's Blues Band and regularly played the Thomas A Becket pub. My old headmaster, Andy Mathieson, was the front man of the band then. The lead singer of Nine Below Zero used to live just off Fremantle Street.' (Gursel Ramadan)

'Dennis Greaves Darwin buildings' boy.' (Gary Busby)

'The original bass player Peter Clarke and the original drummer Kenny Bradley went to Walworth school in the same year as Dennis Greaves. When Andy left, Dennis took over singing duties, until Mark Feltham joined later to help out on vocals. I also produced Nine Below Zero's first EP at Vineyard Studios, behind the Borough Tube station. I also produced "Live At The Marquee" in 1980. They are much better now musically these days. Mark Feltham is, in my opinion, the best harmonica player in Europe.' (Mickey Modern)

'Their album *Third Degree* had a track called 'East Street SE17', which is the market of the Walworth Road.' (Terry James)

'I used to follow them all over London. Dennis was such a showman. Used to work with Pete Clark the bassist.' (Don Rougvie)

'Gary Wallis, who now drums for Pink Floyd, is a Walworth boy. He didn't play with Nine Below Zero, but he did play with Dennis in the group called The Truth.' (Jackie Wallace)

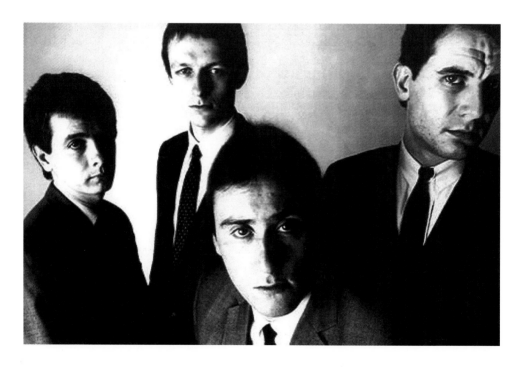

Saturday Morning Pictures

Associated British Cinemas, better known as the ABC, began Saturday morning cinema clubs for children in the 1940s. Those in attendance would sing the 'ABC Minors Song' by following a bouncing ball on the screen that tapped out the lyrics. There would be a main feature, cartoons and competitions to keep everyone in check.

'We used to go to the one at Camberwell. "Flash Gordon" cartoons and then a main film. Then go home and play cowboy and Indians with imaginary horses and guns.' (Tony Lawler)

'My eldest brother used to bunk me in the side door at the Elephant one, so he could keep my entrance money!' (Shirley Till)

'I used to hang around the Wurlitzer organ and had to be in by 9 p.m.' (Patsy Bromley)

'We used to sing "We are the boys and girls well known as Minors of the ABC / And every Saturday all line up / To see the films we like and shout aloud with glee / We like to laugh and have a sing-song /Just a happy crowd are we / Were all pals together / We're minors of the ABC."' (Monique Ballard)

'I won a ticket to go to some kind of special screening. We were all given cuddly elephants to take with us because we were from the Elephant & Castle. I've still got it.' (Susan Gardner)

'I remember watching the Red Hand Gang at the Elephant and getting on stage to dance to win a scratch and sniff T-shirt! Saveloy and chips from Bert's on the way home.' (Nazamin Caffrey)

'I went a few times, and remember bangers being thrown from the gods.' (Andrew Corley)

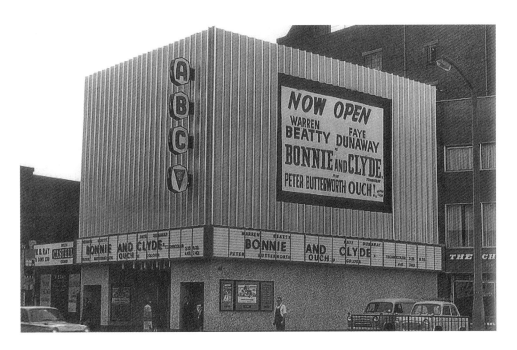

The Blue Rooms

A local club with a distinctively dodgy reputation from the late '50s and early '60s, on the Walworth Road. There was dancing and a bar in there, but reports tell of it being a gambling den, and a place that stolen goods could be obtained. A proper spieler.

'Spent many a happy hour there with some really lovely people.' (Danny Crawley)

'We'd be out all night dancing and walk home with the "west-end tan" – yellow from the nicotine where everyone smoked in the clubs. We'd all walk home over Hungerford Bridge and go to the Blue Rooms in Walworth Road, until it was a decent time to go home having told our parents we were staying at a friends ha! I used to live above Casanova men's shop opposite. Happy days eh?' (Betty Lyons)

'I used Betty's house to get changed, high heels and short skirts, bit of makeup and off we went. A long time ago.' (Judith Adams)

'My dad got told off by my Mum for going there. Something to do with gambling.' (Wendy Rodgers Pocknell)

'It was not only for gambling, it was a place for dancing, which most of us youngsters went there.' (Les Allen)

'I wish I could make time stand still and turn the clocks back to the '50s and '60s and meet all you guys and girls, and show the kids of today how to party and enjoy ourselves without a hint of trouble boy. Oh boy, what great days. The best ever.' (Ray Churchill)

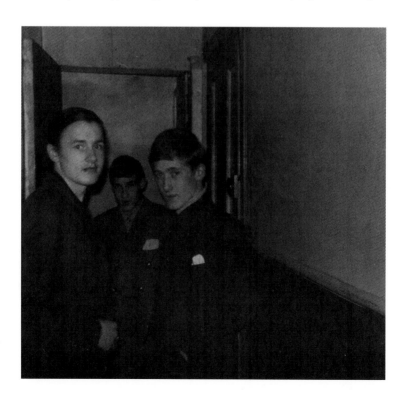

Chapter Ten

In My Childhood Days

Teddy Boys

Inspired by dandies of the Edwardian era, this youth subculture began in the early 1950s. Many involved in the scene often had a violent reputation and there were regular clashes among rival gangs, as well as later being involved in the race riots of Notting Hill in 1958. The 'Teds' of Elephant and Castle tore out cinema seats at screenings of the film *Blackboard Jungle* in order to dance to 'Rock Around The Clock' by Bill Haley and The Comets, which was on the soundtrack. The Teddy boy name is credited to the *Daily Express*, who shortened it from Edwardian to 'Teddy boy'.

'Edwardians wore smart suits of charcoal or clerical grey with 16" bottoms, no turn-ups. Single-breasted jackets with slanted pockets and 'slim Jim' ties. Teds came later and had more distinctive outfits with drape jackets with velvet collars and brothel creeper shoes.' (Fred Waite)

'My mum always mentioned Teddy boys when I was growing up. I thought she was joking when I was little but they were definitely so cool!' (Oz Eryeler)

'My brothers were Teddy boys and I loved their outfits. I went to see Bill Haley at The Trocodero at the Elephant. Amazing show, we were all jiving in the aisles.' (Shirley Ivins)

'They didn't only dance in the aisles. The seats were ripped out to make more room. Rows and rows of them. It was done at Buddy Holly shows as well, I know. I was there.' (Mick Collins)

'I was there too on the night they tore the seats out to jive to Bill Haley and The Comets. I loved them, they were my favourite, even to this day.' (Pat Appleton)

'South London coolness!' (Lucy Dawkins)

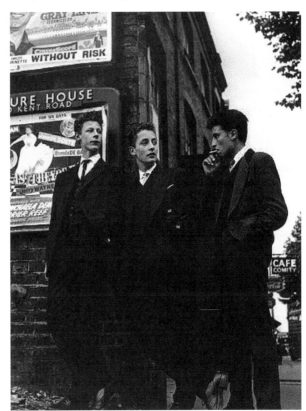

Record Shops

Music played a huge part in the lives of the young, with the advent of rock 'n' roll in the sixties and seventies, pop thereafter. Many old shops, where the latest discs could be bought, are part of the history of those who grew up around them.

'Sundown records, Walworth Road is the one where I spent most of my teenage money.' (Robbie Temple)

'I have a very vivid memory of Harlequin Records having a massive display for "Rocket Man" in the window, so that would make it 1972.' (Rich Rootes)

'I bought a Dansette in the Co-op, Walworth Road, together with three singles. "A Fool Such As I" – Elvis, "It Doesn't Matter Anymore" – Buddy Holly and "Smoke Gets In Your Eyes" – The Platters. About 1959 I think?' (Richard Mann)

'We had a red Dansette, but only two records for a long time. Johnny Ray and Slim Whitman. Drove my dad mad!' (Barbara Brown)

'Mr and Mrs Levy worked on the A1 stall and we used to put the Top 40 on the record player. Mrs Levy used to scratch the life out of a record when she took it off. I used give my wages back to them by buying most of the stock that weekend, but it set me up in my DJ'ing business.' (Neil Howie Aylward)

'I worked on the record counter at A1 for a year or so around 1970. Melvyn was the son involved on records. I remember the listening booths at the back of the shop – such a funny idea!' (Jill Hawkins)

'I was offered a job sweeping up in there around 1962 to support my vinyl habit, but homework and, more importantly, playing football, were much more important to me.' (Terry Edwards)

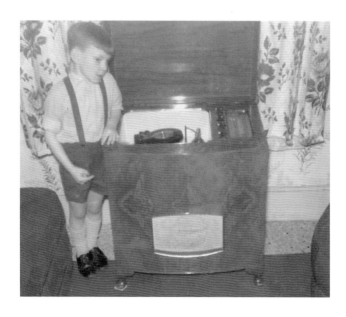

Sweet Shops

Another right of passage, and a time when you were allowed to spend your own money. Because you had limited funds, it was a tough decision what to spend it on though? Within a short while, however, most of us had our favourites.

'I'd always get a Jubbly after school.₁' (Steve Gray)

'I used to share my Jubbly with my friend. Not very hygienic I know, but I'm still here to tell the tale!' (Denise Fox)

'Do you remember that sweetshop in the "Lane" by Blackwood Street? Had its ice cream fridge outside. They sold Everest lollies, Push Ups and Screwballs.' (Michele Hailey)

'I used to get my green jelly snakes at a penny each. Always spent my bus fare. I then walked home instead, worth every footstep.' (Linda Nimmo McTernan)

'Old Marie from our block would get me to go and get her ten "Number 6" fags and tell me to spend the change. I was only eight!' (Dave Baxter)

'If the stick of your ice lolly had writing on it you got another free!' (Monica Harrison)

'Remember "Potato Puffs"? You couldn't buy them anywhere else!' (Jo Cater)

'Oh yeah. Salt and vinegar were great, but barbecue flavour were the guvnors.' (Keith Ilsey)

'Smaller size than Wotsits but similar shape, made of a light crisp. Keith, I agree, there were quite a few flavours.' (Danny Walters)

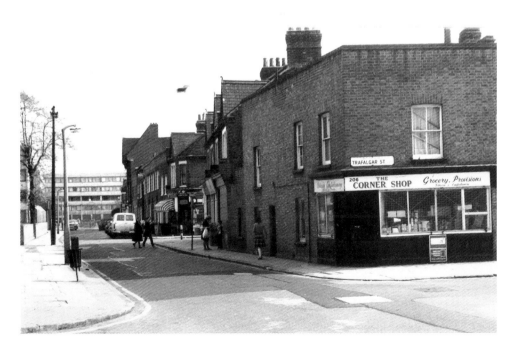

Christmas

No run up to Christmas Day was complete without a visit to 'Santa's Grotto' in a department store, like Jones and Higgins, which was situated in nearby Peckham. There you would be taken to have your photograph done with 'Santa' and would be given a little present. Nearly everyone we spoke to had one of those photos and great memories.

'I used to go to Jones and Higgins to see Father Christmas in his grotto, every year as a kid.' (Mark Bourne)

'I remember the Father Christmas train and the moving scenery. It was so amazing that it is still one of my best Christmas memories.' (Pam King)

'I bet we all sat in the Santa train together at some point, all those years ago. I thought I was travelling for miles ha ha. I never dreamt it was the scenery moving.' (Maggie Webb)

'I remember seeing Father Christmas in there and then going into the tearooms over the road after. I was very young and impressed at being served by woman in white aprons. Think it was Lyons Tea House?' (Debbie Townsend Wright)

'Visited that every year with my Godparents and then went for my favourite cake – pineapple ring, sponge, fresh cream, coated in chocolate.' (Caroline Little)

'My dad always took my brother and myself over to Hamleys around Christmas time, I loved going there.' (Brenda Cooper)

'That was very posh Brenda! I had to make do with Peckham!' (Christine McQuade)

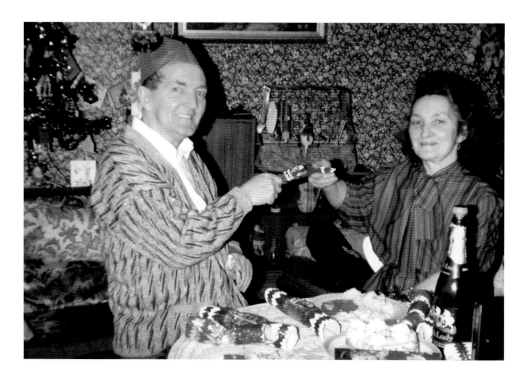

Faraday Gardens

Local play area named after Michael Faraday, a leader in the field of electro mechanics who was born locally. The gardens were built on Church Commissioners' land in 1905. An air-raid shelter stood here in the Second World War. It is a popular park for dog walkers and children to this day.

'I remember when they had barrage balloons in that park.' (Jean Yeo)

'We lived in the top flat in the first block on the right until I was about fourteen. We looked out to a large play area and behind were the swings, a slide and a roundabout. Behind that, St Peter's School was to the left and to the right, the back gardens of the houses in Trafalgar Street. There was also a park keeper and his hut.' (Valerie Simmonds)

'This was our sports ground when I was at St Peters.' (Brenda Jordan)

'There were no gardens there then. Pure concrete swing park and football pitch. I remember balancing along that wall, and trying to jump across the gaps!' (Michele Hailey)

'That was our football pitch, cricket ground, roller-skating and carting stadium. We often had to climb the fence into the back gardens of Trafalgar Street, or the backyards of Liverpool Grove, to get the ball. Sharing a drag on a "Tuppenny Weight", showing off to the girls on the swings and trying to persuade the park keeper to leave it open just a little longer.' (Richard Mann)

'I spent many a happy hour there playing football and generally mucking about, no doubt annoying the "parkie". We called him "Chewfag" because he always had a cigarette hanging out of his mouth.' (Robin Page)

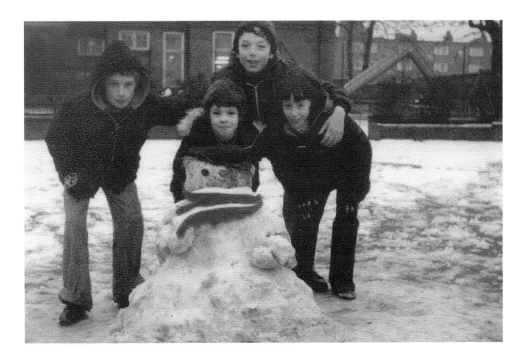

The Boys' Brigade

This was the first uniformed organization for the British youth. It was started in 1883 by William A. Smith in Scotland. Its objectives were: 'To help Boys develop and grow in Christian character. To train Boys to become loyal and responsible citizens and to promote boys' physical fitness and develop their leadership potential.' Its motto is 'Sure and Steadfast'.

'The 168 Boys Brigade were based at the East Street Baptist church.' (James Webb)

'I was in the BB based in the old chapel right across the road from where I lived in Wells Way, but we also met in Brunswick Park School for parade drill, in the hall in winter and in the yard in summer. Being Catholics we were supposed to go to the scouts, but they were based way over in Rodney Road. Good way to get to know more local kids.' (Nick Sweeney)

'Leslie Worm and Henry Quennell were two of the boys who played the bugle on the roof on Remembrance Sundays in the '50s.' (Pat Collins)

'My husband, John Woolley, was in the 4th London, this was in early '70s – all long hair and flares. He went as far as lieutenant, then went to East Street 168, where he became captain.' (Deborah Woolley)

'The B.B. song: "You can't go wrong, there you learn the music, to keep your body strong, why don't you be one of us, and join our happy throng, we will welcome you, and teach you to sing our B.B. song."' (Billy Sinclair)

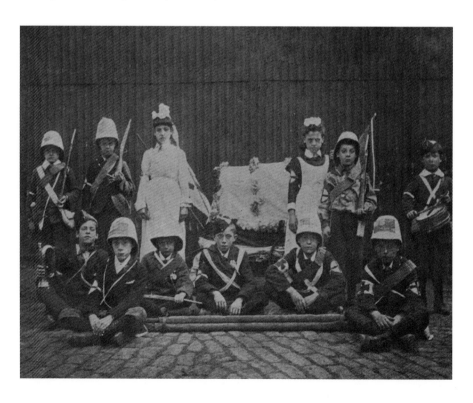

School Uniforms

Generations of boys and girls from the immediate area all got their uniforms from Whitehall Clothiers, at No. 77 Camberwell Road. The shop also gained notoriety in the 1980s as a supplier of expensive Italian sportswear that was very popular among the 'casual' youth cult.

'I was always knew it was near the end of the summer when my mum dragged me down there for my uniform!' (Maddie Wallace-Collier)

'I bought my son's first school trousers there; he's 53 now.' (Pauline Townsend)

'Will, the owner, found me a tiny Bacon blazer for my son Craig as he was only about the size of a 7-year-old when started there. The old linen style was much smarter.' (Nicole Bolt)

'I got my Silverthorne uniform there. I was a tiny girl, but I had to have large blazer so "I'd grow into it." It was still too big 5 years later!' (Carole Bolton)

'I got my maroon Walworth School uniform there. Back in the day, we had the pink-and-white check blouse.' (Shelley Rosher)

'I worked there from 1978 to about 1984. Will has been there many years and still there now, nicest man I have ever met.' (Chris Foley)

'I bought my eldest a "Lacoste" polo shirt there in the early '80s, cost a flaming fortune! They had queues down the street buying Fila this and Diadorra that.' (Jean Baxter)

'I bought some smart reversible bright coloured trousers in there. "Miami Vice" was the fashion at that time. Bit sad now.' (Darren Bolton)

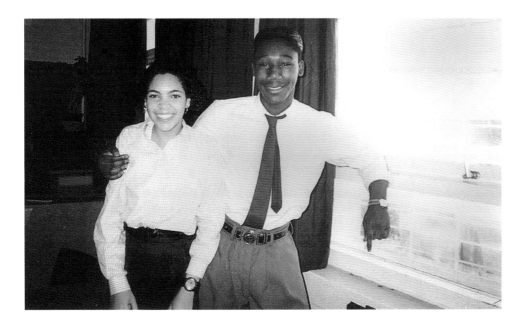

Arments Special

Arments' Anniversary

'Roy and I would like to say a big thank you to all of you who have wished us a happy birthday and thank those of you who joined in our celebration day. Also a special thank you to all of our staff for working so hard to make our Centenary celebration a day to remember; you did a tremendous job and we are very fortunate to have such good, loyal people work for us.' (Cheryl Arment)

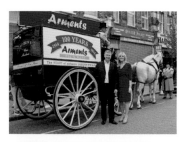
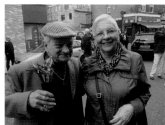
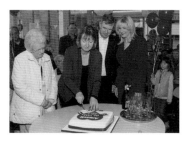

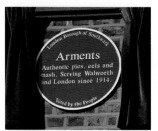
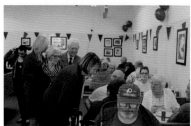
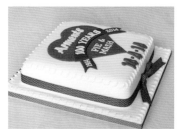

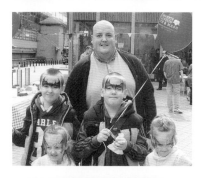
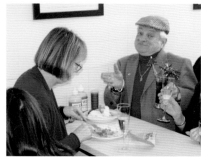
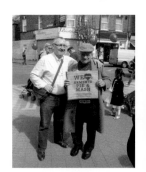

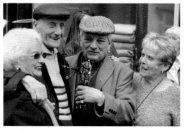
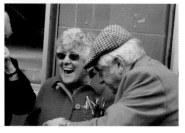
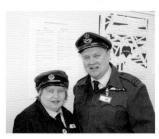